11/13/95

Ontological
Commitment

Philosophy Conference, 3d, University
of Georgia, 1970

ONTOLOGICAL COMMITMENT

Edited by
RICHARD H. SEVERENS

University of Georgia Press
Athens

Library of Congress Catalog Card Number: 73–76785
International Standard Book Number: 0–8203–0335–6

The University of Georgia Press, Athens 30602

Printed in the United States of America

CONTENTS

1891333

PREFACE

The essays in this volume were presented at the third annual Philosophy Conference held on April 2–4, 1970, sponsored by the University of Georgia Department of Philosophy. (The papers comprising the first two conferences have been published previously by the University of Georgia Press as *Religious Language and Knowledge* and *Education and Ethics*.) As in the earlier conferences, philosophers from several universities were invited to present papers on a topic of perennial concern. The 1970 conference focused on the issue of ontological commitment, a classical issue which is now enjoying considerable contemporary interest. The resulting essays reflect several different approaches to this topic.

Ontology, or the inquiry as to what there is, has traditionally been regarded as a major branch of philosophical investigation. Indeed, it has sometimes been regarded as the primary philosophical subject—all other philosophical issues depending ultimately upon ontological issues. The ontological commitments of our sundry statements—those purported entities which must exist if the statements are to be true—become crucially important in the inquiry as to what there is. For this reason philosophers endeavor to analyze carefully and explicate those statements. The present volume contributes to that continuing analysis and explication.

Willard Van Orman Quine brought the notion of ontological commitment into clear contemporary focus with his now-famous criterion of ontological commitment. It will be obvious that several of the essays comprising the present volume owe much of their inspiration to him. But the scope of these essays ranges well beyond consideration of Quine's criterion alone. They diverge in method, purpose, and topic. Yet whether they query the ontological commitments which appear to be implicit in our uses of language or whether they delve into the notion of ontological commitment itself, they share a common concern.

The essays divide themselves naturally into two sorts. Three of the essays, 1, 4, and 5, deal directly with the concept of ontological commitment, sometimes in ways congenial to Quine's criterion, sometimes not. In essay 4 we find what is essentially an emendation of Quine's criterion for ontological commitment. Essay 5 traces lucidly the evolution of Quine's criterion, and, in general, defends that criterion. In essay 1, on the other hand, there is exhibited a generally skeptical attitude toward Quine's criterion—and any criterion like it—throughout its evolution.

Essay 2 is devoted largely to the question whether our use of adverbial modifiers involves an irrevocable ontological commitment to events, conceived as irreducible entities. In essay 3 there is inquiry into the question of ontological commitment to a deity, particularly by way of examining the traditional Ontological Argument with a view to exposing its ontological force.

In essay 6 there is a discussion of events from the point of view of the philosophy of history in an attempt to analyze the ontological status of "events" and related concepts, such as "the past" and "history." While the problems associated with our ontological commitments to objects, numbers, and other would-be entities have received considerable attention in recent years, philosophers have sometimes overlooked the question whether we are committed to events.

Although the essays are arranged in the order in which they were initially presented, they could be grouped differently since essays 1, 4, and 5 might be regarded as basically methodological in character, while essays 2, 3, and 6 might be regarded as substantive in character.

It will be obvious that there is no general agreement on the issues raised in this volume. If there were agreement, this volume would not have been necessary. Illustrative of this lack of agreement are both the question whether events are to be postulated as required by way of partial explanation of facts of our experience, and the question what constitutes ontological commitment in the first place. Both questions, as well as many related ones, remain open.

The hard fact is that there are large differences as to what constitutes ontological commitment, as well as to what a given statement or theory commits its author. This volume, it is hoped, makes vivid some of those differences.

Richard H. Severens

NOTES ON CONTRIBUTORS

John Beversluis is assistant professor of philosophy at Butler University. His primary interest is in the area of epistemology.

Robert G. Burton is assistant professor of philosophy at the University of Georgia. His areas of special interest are metaphysics, epistemology, and the philosophy of science.

L. B. Cebik is associate professor of philosophy at the University of Tennessee. He is the author of several essays in metaphysics and philosophy of history.

Charles S. Chihara is assistant professor of philosophy at the University of California at Berkeley. He is the author of several essays on the topic of ontological commitment.

Romane Clarke is professor of philosophy at Indiana University. Author of a number of articles in the area of logic and language, Professor Clarke is coauthor of *An Introduction to Logic*.

Bowman L. Clarke is professor of philosophy and head of the Department of Philosophy at the University of Georgia. He is the author of numerous articles in the areas of epistemology and metaphysics, and of *Language and Natural Theology*.

James F. Harris, Jr., is assistant professor of philosophy at the College of William and Mary. He is author of *Ethics and Academics* and coeditor of *Analyticity*.

John Heintz is assistant professor of philosophy at the University of Alberta. His primary interests are in the areas of logic, epistemology, and metaphysics.

Scott A. Kleiner is assistant professor of philosophy at the University of Georgia. Professor Kleiner's interests are primarily in the area of the history and philosophy of science.

James W. Oliver is professor of philosophy at the University of South Carolina. He is the author of a number of articles in the areas of logic and epistemology.

Richard H. Severens is associate professor of philosophy at the University of Georgia. He is the author of several articles in the areas of epistemology and metaphysics and is coeditor of *Analyticity*.

Robert Vorsteg is assistant professor of philosophy at Wake Forest University.

CHANNELING COMMITMENTS
Richard H. Severens

Quine's[1] justly celebrated criterion of ontological commitment, though already much discussed, has not diminished in philosophical interest over the passing years. Indeed, its very durability is sufficient to justify its reassessment, such being the fate of celebrated doctrines. His criterion, telling us, as it purportedly does, how to tell what there is according to any given theory or declaration generally, proves for the moment to be an indispensable tool for metaphysical investigations. Because it is justly celebrated, it should not be necessary to rehearse that criterion here. But it may be instructive to reflect momentarily upon what the criterion itself commits us to. For in passively accepting any given criterion for ontological commitment, we may well commit ourselves in other ways: ways which we may later actively wish to avoid. Thus it is that Quine's criterion of ontological commitment deserves further scrutiny and prompts the following reflections. For example, Quine's criterion enjoins us to commit ourselves to view ontological commitment as directed through a single channel: linguistic reference by means of the variables of quantification. The bound variables of quantification achieve this high office by default, as it were, since all other devices for reference, particularly singular reference, are resolvable in familiar fashion: they disappear under analysis and the bound variables take up their referential duties. Singular terms, so the argument goes, are thus theoretically superfluous. There are three main morals to be drawn from this account, sketchy almost to the point of caricature, of Quine's criterion. And although it is probably gratuitous actually to draw them, doing so will provide a fixed reference for what is to follow. First, there is *one* channel of ontological commitment. Second, that channel is linguistic reference. And third, the vehicle of that reference is the bound variable.[2] Such are some at least of the commitments to which one binds oneself in opting for Quine's criterion of ontological commitment. And it is these latter commitments which provoke the following ruminations.

I

Initially the most striking aspect of Quine's criterion is its divergence from what might have been expected from anything that is represented as being our criterion of ontological commitment. For if we take that criterion literally, then what we get by way of commitments is something radically different from what tradition would have led us to await. When we consider what entities are, in fact, the values of the variables in our usual statements, we come up, for example, with broken ashtrays and rotten turnips. Yet the dedicated ontologist is ordinarily not much concerned with broken ashtrays and rotten turnips, and would be much surprised to discover that he unwittingly was. Of course, we may also encounter sense data and attributes amongst the values of our bound variables, but there is no need for encountering them and their ilk to the exclusion of ashtrays and turnips. And anyway we do so encounter ashtrays and turnips.

This circumstance is aggravated when the bound variable in question is appended to an adjectival predicate such as 'green' or a verb such as 'runs', as opposed to a substantive such as 'ashtray' or 'turnip'. For then, lacking further information not supplied by the criterion, we have commitment to a green one and one that runs. Being committed to a green one or to a running one is not something that would ordinarily exercise those interested in ontology. The pressing question, not answered by the criterion, is: "A green *what*?" And this should lead us to wonder, at least in many cases, whether the criterion does in fact tell us what there is. When the predicate affixed to the variable in question is any one of a large number of adjectives and verbs, for example 'green', 'rotten', 'runs', and so on, the criterion does not tell us what, over and above runners and green ones, we are committed to. It does not even tell us, for example, whether we are committed to martians as opposed to avocados, or sprinters as opposed to cheetahs.

Now a Quinean might find this situation a curiosity but not at all disturbing: the criterion remains intact despite the oddity. Another Quinean, concerned about calling his criterion "ontological," might try a different strategy. He might argue that the criterion is applicable when one is speaking with the learned, but not when speaking with the vulgar. In other words the criterion is brought to bear only on theoretical, or otherwise esoteric, discourse. Ashtrays and turnips thus appropriately excluded, we can return contentedly to our sense data and attributes.

There are three reasons why this strategy fails. First, it is simply ad hoc, and this is reflected in the fact that it presupposes an already intelligible distinction between what is esoteric and what is not. Where, exactly, to draw the line remains to be seen, and it is likely that the difference is a matter of degree—that there is no line to be drawn. Second, even the most esoteric discourse will often include bound variables taking mundane objects as their values. For example, variables taking, say, thermometers or other experimental apparatus or even mathematical marks for their values are appropriate cases. And even our discourse about sense data is liberally laced with variables having commerce with colors, shapes, and bad smells. And third, the strategy does not solve the apparent difficulty which arose when the text appended to the variable is an adjective rather than a common noun.

Quine himself seems to be more nearly the second type of Quinean than the first; that is, he takes the word 'ontological' seriously. Indeed, he envisions a world composed of physical objects and classes only. That this is what he is committed to we are to discover by checking the values of his variables. Aside from a few specific occurrences of 'physical object' and 'class' appended to bound variables in true statements, which hardly accomplish Quine's purpose, the bulk of the values of the variables will be of the general ilk of ashtrays and turnips. And if there is a lesson to be learned from Berkeley and Hume, it is a very long way from ashtrays and turnips to physical objects. Quine's criterion alone does not tell us that his world is a world of physical objects and classes only: we need collateral information. Similarly, a subsidiary argument is needed to rescue classes from being mere aggregates of turnips, and so on. So the criterion seems, at least, to be insufficient to identify the *ontological* commitments of a theory, Quine's included.

The transition from such mundane entities as ashtrays and

turnips to what might be called "proper" ontological entities, such as physical objects or universals for example, is the point at which ontological commitment obtrudes itself on the scene.[3] (Very few, after all, would deny that there are ashtrays and turnips.) For the mundane objects may receive different constructions under differing conceptual schemes, and statements about them may have differing implications under differing conceptual schemes. Whether the turnip is to become a physical object or a collection of sense data depends upon the machinery of the conceptual scheme in question. Ontological commitment thus is a matter far more complicated than the criterion suggests, and the role played by bound variables is at best only a part of the whole. We need, for example, to know which conceptual scheme is involved. (Indeed, it is greatly to be wondered whether we do not need already to know what its ontology is.) In any case, there seems to be a good deal more to the story than quantification over variables.

2

Quine's criterion is framed *within* the context of the logic of quantification. It tells us, that is, how to determine ontological commitments when the statements to be investigated have been rendered in the language of quantification. But, ironically, Quine, among others, has shown how we can do without the language of quantification: how we can do without the whole apparatus of quantifiers and the variables which they bind.[4] This alternative system may, for convenience, be called the "language of combinators." Since quantifiers and variables have both disappeared in the latter, something other than Quine's criterion must, in the language of combinators, determine ontological commitments. Two points emerge. First, the language of combinators contains only certain logical operators, on the one hand, and predicates on the other. And this, in turn, suggests two things: that we might profit by looking toward predicates in search of a criterion of ontological commitment, and that reference by means of variables, or any other sort of referring device for that matter, may not be the key to the criterion sought. Second, Quine's criterion is, at best, relative to the mode in which we choose to express ourselves.

As before, a Quinean could protest that, relative or not, Quine's criterion does the job as far as the language employing quantifiers and variables is concerned, and since that language is good enough for the vast bulk of what we wish to express, it is good enough for us. Hardly anything more could be asked of any criterion of ontological commitment. But this admirably succinct reply makes the matter appear more simple than it really is. For the relativity of Quine's criterion may well be taken as showing that that criterion really does not get to the bottom of things as far as ontological commitment is concerned: it is merely the reflection, *in quantification*, of a more general notion. That is, Quine's criterion may be a *mark* of ontological commitment so far as quantification is concerned, but it is not an *analysis* of that notion. And a very modest Quinean might even acquiesce in this. But we still have not pressed the matter far enough.

For it does no good to protest that, even though the criterion is a mere symptom, rather than an analysis, of ontological commitment, its relativity is still no impediment. That is, having somehow fashioned a criterion of commitment for the language of combinators, we would find that the same discourse would have the same commitments, no matter which of the systems was the vehicle of its expression. For the language of combinators may well be by no means the only alternative to the language of quantifiers and variables. There may indeed be a multitude of further alternatives. And to know that their criteria yield just those commitments that Quine's criterion yields would seem to require knowing the *analysis* of the notion of ontological commitment. At least so it would appear. Modesty is not always profitable.

Of course, we could still check the alternatives one by one against the language of quantifiers and variables, and even be pleasantly surprised to find no divergence of commitments. But to do this would be to betray initial doubts about Quine's criterion, even as a *mark* of commitment.

On the other hand, if Quine's criterion is meant to be the analysis (for quantification) of ontological commitment, then its relativity shows that it is just one criterion of (possibly) many, and the reason that we prize it is simply that we happen to be Quantificationalists, rather in the way that an Austrian is an Austrian. We Quantificationalists use as our symptom of ontological commitment the one proffered by Quine. But just as our erstwhile

Austrian might just as well have been a Yugoslav, so also we
might just as well have been Combinatorians, regarding the Quantificationalists as the eccentric minority. Indeed, it is surely an historical accident that we learned our logic at the knee of Gottlob
Frege rather than that of Moses Schonfinkel,[5] the inventor of the
logic of combinators. But the matter is even more striking than
this. For just as the logic of combinators *might* never have been
invented, so likewise, the logic of quantifiers and variables might
never have been invented. Thus transient is Quine's criterion.

One final point already mentioned and to which we shall presently recur: the logic of combinators has as vocabulary the combinators themselves and predicates. In looking for ontological
commitments, our attention is thus naturally drawn toward the
predicates.

3

There is something just a little spooky admixed with the hard-
headed good sense of Quine's criterion. It is a mere suspicion
rather than a clear fact, and its haunting quality is nearly obscured
by the intuitive appeal of Quine's criterion. But it is there, nagging,
nonetheless. It is clear that Quine did not simply pull his criterion
rabbit-fashion out of a mixed bag of maxims, nor did he enact it
like an absolute monarch. Rather, the criterion is the product of
careful philosophical work. The question then is what would lead
one to discover a criterion for ontological commitment. How
would one tell when one in fact had hit upon it? What would count
as evidence that what one had discovered was an infallible mark
of ontological commitment? One could already know the ontological commitments of some theory, and then simply figure out
what announced them. And this is the source of the nagging
suspicion: that looking for the marks first, and then for the commitments later, is procedurally backward. More precisely, looking first for the syntactical devices which channel commitment,
and later for the commitments themselves is logically in reverse.
How is it possible, it might reasonably be asked, to identify the
committing devices without already knowing, for one theory at
least, what its commitments actually are?

It thus appears initially that Quine's criterion comes after the
fact. Why not, for example, say that a theory or statement is

committed to just those entities whose mention occurs immediately after a preposition; such a view might even be construed as reminiscent of the doctrine of internal relations. Or, to pile absurdity upon absurdity, why not say that parentheses are the vehicles of commitment? It would seem that the only way in which such questions are to be resolved is to have in mind what the commitments of a given theory are before determining the linguistic vehicles of those commitments, which, in turn, suggests that the assignment of certain linguistic devices as vehicles of commitment is logically posterior to determining the commitments in question, in some other way, for at least one theory.

The phrase 'there is . . .' which is the usual correlate in English of the existential quantifier, has the reassuring virtue of imputing existence, or seemingly so, and thus, the quantifier and its variables, as opposed to parentheses, seem to be the proper vehicles of commitment. And it might be argued that this fact justifies their selection as the devices of commitment, and that this selection does not depend upon the prior determination of the actual commitments of some theory. We can avoid the reverse logic, it might be argued, just because we can understand the quantifier and the function of its variables.

But this argument simply will not do. For there are myriad uses of 'there is . . .' and its variants, in which the imputation of existence, is either tactitly or explicitly to be withheld. For example, 'there is a rattlesnake right behind you' uttered by a prankster unmindful of the fact that there is one there is such a case. Our prankster may be speaking frivolously, but he is not speaking untruthfully. And so are 'if it is both raining and not raining then there are basilisks,' and 'whether or not there are unicorns, either it is raining or it is not.' Many like examples could be produced. These are all truths in which there is no commitment to rattlesnakes, basilisks, and unicorns. Switching, if it is fair, to the subjunctive mood, 'if there were such a thing as Dracula, then he would enjoy blood sausage' is a case of the explicit withholding of the imputation of existence. Whether or not the switch is fair is another question. In any case, we seem to have uncovered cases of truths in which the phrase 'there is . . .' does not carry the imputation of existence, cases in which we would claim we were not committed to basilisks and their ilk. And there are further cases. Such is 'there is a spy in this room', uttered truly, but without knowledge, by one who wishes to break up a meeting. 'If snow is black, then there is a solution to Fermat's Last Theorem' might well be used to affirm that there is no such solution. And so on and on. The phrase 'there is . . .' is thus not a sure guide to the imputation of existence, and hence, any criterion which trades on its existential force is weakened. So the argument whereby the existential quantifier and its variables carry commitment, insofar as it draws its force from 'there is . . .' is likewise weakened. And thus the most promising alternative to the reversal recently mentioned fails.

But these dark musings must be interrupted, for we have other business to attend to.

4

We have thus far been speculating on what might be called "inconveniences" encountered in Quine's criterion. We need now to inquire whether there are any positive reasons for shying away from it. Any criterion of ontological commitment must itself be ontologically neutral; it must treat equally all of the candidates for which ontological status might be claimed. It must, thus, be such as not to rule out any ontological possibilities in advance. It must not, that is, exclude ontological contenders, solely by being the kind of criterion it is. And likewise it must not enforce commitment to entities of a certain sort, simply because of the sort of criterion it is. With this in mind, let us take a second look at Quine's criterion. We noted earlier that, according to that criterion, ontological commitment is directed through the bound variables of the theory or statement in question. The medium of commitment is linguistic reference. Thus anything to which we *can* be committed must be a referent. But what if it is responsibly argued that there are entities to which reference cannot significantly be made? What, in other words, of entities to which we may be irreferentially committed?

There are two cases which come to mind in this (possible) emergency. First, Frege[6] distinguished carefully between what he called "objects" and what he called "concepts." The principal point of difference was that expressions for objects could meaningfully flank the identity sign, while expressions for concepts could not. Thus, while 'Ned = Jed' is grammatically (and logically) acceptable, 'friendly = congenial' is not. It is not the case that friendly is identical to congenial, though it is, perhaps, the case that friendliness is identical to congeniality. 'Friendly' and 'congenial' "stand for" concepts, while 'friendliness' and 'congeniality' refer to objects. In Fregean terms, 'friendliness' and 'congeniality' are "saturated" (can express a complete idea by themselves), while 'friendly' and 'congenial' are "unsaturated" (do not express complete ideas, one needs to know *what* is friendly, and so on). Concepts, according to Frege, cannot thus be *named*. They are related to discourse in another way. This is, of course, not to deny the trivial thesis that anybody can use almost anything as a name for a given entity; rather, it is to affirm the nontrivial thesis that such names merely serve by fiat as stand-ins for the expressions (nonnames) which stand for concepts. (This may suggest a way of resolving the familiar Fregean paradox 'the concept *horse* is not a concept', the phrase 'the concept *horse*' being merely an ersatz way of bringing the concept into the discussion.) The only *real* grip which language has on concepts is through such expressions as ' . . . is a horse'. Concepts, on Frege's view, are thus not nameable. It is but a short step, confirmed by the relation between naming and other modes of reference (Frege's paradox uses a definite description, not a name), to the conclusion that concepts cannot significantly be referred to at all, save by ersatz fly-by-nights. Thus they cannot significantly be the values of bound variables, the latter being, as noted, the ultimate vehicles of reference. We *cannot*, therefore, be committed to concepts, even though we have responsibile arguments, wrong though they may be, that concepts are a part of what we are committed to ontologically. So Quine's criterion simply begs the question against Frege. By its commitment to the view that commitment is essentially referential, it excludes concepts before their case has even been heard. Thus it apparently fails.

Another equally good case is that of Everett Hall.[7] He argued that there are facts, and he argued that facts cannot be named. Again, this is not to deny the trivial thesis that anybody can use anything he wishes to use as a name for anything. Rather, it is to assert the nontrivial thesis that the relation between fact and language is not the name-relation. And whatever purports to be the name of a fact is merely an artifice pretending to name while really expressing some other relation. We may, without doing too much violence to Hall, say that names name things while sentences assert facts. It is the relation of asserting or stating, not naming, which holds between language and fact.

Because of the more obvious interrelations between the various devices for reference, and also because of Hall's apparent intentions, his argument may be extended so as to conclude that significant (as opposed to ersatz) reference to facts simply cannot be made.

It is thus that facts *cannot* be values of variables, whether there are any facts or not. Quine's criterion thus makes commitment to facts impossible, and makes it impossible in advance.

So, we have apparently two cases in which Quine's criterion simply fails. It fails, not by admitting nonexistents, nor by failing to admit entities to which commitment is made, but by making it *impossible* for there to be commitment to putative entities to which we *may* be committed.

Now, of course, Hall and Frege may both be utterly wrong. But, even if they are, that fact is completely beside the point. The fact is that both have argued responsibly for their views, and those views are, on the surface at least, internally consistent. But Quine's criterion rules them out unheard. Moreover, it rules them out on the basis of the utterly unproved principle that reference is the *only* access that language has to reality, the *only* channel through which commitment may occur. Indeed, these misgivings are merely a reflection of a more general one, namely that there may be many channels of commitment, which *may* be indicated by the fact that the assumption remains unproved. We have already noted the reassuringly existential ring of the phrase 'there is . . .' and this may lie behind the assumption. But we have also noted that the ring may not be as reassuring as it seems. And there is involved the further assumption that linguistic reference carries existential import, in the first place, which assumption may well prove dangerous. But we shall return to this intriguing topic later.

5

It was ironic enough that Quine himself should have shown us one way to get along without any variables and quantifiers at all. But it is even more ironic that other work of Quine's should *suggest* a possible alternative, within quantification, to his criterion. It will be recalled that our attention was drawn especially in section 2 to a possibly important role which predicates may play in the matter of ontological commitment. Quine actually does us one better.[8] For it does not unduly distort his work, I think, to construe it in the following way. He shows how all of the bound variables may be so mustered as to be opaque as to what they commit us to. In order to *standardize* a theory or a segment of discourse, the variables are aggregated in such a way as to make any context meaningful for any variable. There results a single style of variables, ranging alike over any kind of entity whatever. This is accomplished, in effect, by relativizing the copula. By varying, as the occasion demands, the interpretation of the copula, the goal of *standardization* can be achieved. Where we have the truth, for example, that x is y, and y is a class, then 'is' is to be interpreted as 'is a member of' or 'is included in', and where y is an attribute, 'is' has the force of 'exemplifies' or 'is an instance of', and so on. Examples of this sort could be multiplied at will.

The variables themselves remain mute as to what they commit us to; that job is left to the copula. The idea is that the variables may be herded together to do their main job—serving to show what is being said about what—while the kinds of things about which anything is said, is indicated by the copula used, or more properly, the required interpretation of the copula in any given case (this gives a further thrust to the dark musings of section 3). The variables, in effect, tell us nothing, while the copula tells us everything, about what the theory or segment of discourse in question commits us to.

This, if it is a fair representation of Quine's result, suggests a new criterion of ontological commitment. Take a given theory or segment of discourse, *standardize* it, separate its (purported) truths, and note the various interpretations of the copula required. The ontological commitments of the theory will be reflected in those interpretations. Thus, where 'is a member of' or 'is included in' (in their set-theoretic sense) is required, the theory will be committed to classes. And where 'exemplifies' is required, the theory will be committed to attributes.

At least we have the beginnings of a criterion here, and one which depresses the role played by the variables, while emphasizing the role played by predicates.

Anachronism sometimes being the price of dramatic effect, it should be pointed out that Wang[9] had already achieved a result substantially similar to Quine's *standardization*. For our purposes, Wang's strategy may be put roughly as follows: a certain stock of predicates is selected and prefixed conditionally to the various statements of the theory in such a way as to specify what the bound variables in those statements range over, thus eliminating the need to segregate the variables into separate styles. This sketch, inadequate and oversimplified though it is, illustrates in another way the importance of predicates relative to variables. Once again an alternative criterion of commitment is suggested. Having separated out the purported truths of the theory, we simply check which predicates are needed to achieve the single style of variables. And these will tell us its ontological commitments.

Whether either of these criteria will bear up under careful scrutiny remains in question. But they do, initially at least, suggest that certain predicates may have a more important role in ontological commitment than do quantifiers and their variables.

It should be noted that both of these alternatives are subject to the misgivings entertained in section 4. But they may not be subject to those of section 1. That is, it may well be that we can avoid the ashtrays and turnips in favor of sense data and universals, for example, or come up with a criterion that represents the theory as trafficking in physical objects and classes, while discoursing of ashtrays and piles of turnips. And the fact that they are subject to those of section 3, may be taken as tending to confirm that section. For selecting which predicates or which copulas to use in the first place would suggest that we already have knowledge of the ontological commitments of some theory, and are attempting to frame a criterion to square with that knowledge. But we have further, more chancy, issues awaiting us.

6

We have, thus far, confined ourselves to relatively safe areas of inquiry: it is time now to adopt a more venturesome spirit, and to move into some less well charted areas. The risk may well prove worth the insight gained. The facile translation of the English idiom 'there is . . .' into the existential quantifier, carrying the usual existential import of 'there is . . .' over into quantification, is apparently the move which leads to Quine's criterion. But this move is one which may be questioned. We do not seem to be logically compelled to make it. We *could*, conveniently or not, regard the existential quantifier instead as the particular quantifier, answering to the universal quantifier, and doing the duties left undone by the latter. The operation of existential instantiation would then become a means of introducing an unquantified expression to index the relevant predicates and facilitate deduction, while existential generalization would be the means of discharging such expressions.[10] There is no contradiction in supposing the existential quantifier to carry no existential import, unless we are committed in advance to the facile translation mentioned above. And if logic can get along without the latter, why can't we? Indeed, unless we are already committed to the notion that the existential quantifier is possessed of existential import, unless, that is, we are already Quineans, there is no prima facie reason for connecting our existential commitments with the marks '(', '∃', '*x*', ')'. And we noted in section 5, our ontological commitments may well be reflected in other ways.

Moreover, we have already seen that the mere occurrence of the bit 'there is . . .' does not always carry existential import. Our little devices of making occurrences of contexts employing 'there is . . .' the consequents of self-contradictory antecedents, or antecedents of tautologous consequents seemed to show that. So our facile translation is dubious anyway.

The question then arises why and how we can isolate certain statements for preferential treatment. What, in other words, is our guide as to which contexts of 'there is . . .' are bestowed with existential import, and which not? Why, for example, do we shun the subjunctive mood? Just because the criterion does not work there? Why should the indicative mood be granted special privileges in the matter of ontological commitment?

Insofar as the existential quantifier derives its existential force from the familiar 'there is . . .' of English, its credentials are not quite in order.

But there is another source from which the existential quantifier may draw its existential force, and that is from the variables themselves. And this is a matter which needs to be opened up. Variables are referring devices; indeed, if Quine's elimination of singular terms is correct, they are the only remaining referring devices and the only ones necessary. They refer rather in the manner of pronouns: fixing reference but not fixing it specifically. 'It' refers to something, but it doesn't tell *which* thing is referred to, save by virtue, not of itself, but by the text in which it functions as referring device. Likewise, the reference of variables is directed by the predicates to which they are affixed.

Now it is commonplace to regard successful linguistic reference as carrying existential import. How else, it might rhetorically be asked, does language have any grip on the world at all? Of course, linguistic reference may fail: there may exist no entity to which the referring expression in question refers. But it cannot fail in any true statement, another familiar commonplace has it. And this is one of the reasons why Quine's criterion is directed upon purportedly true statements. Thus the existential quantifier becomes existential by virtue of its association with variables which, as referring devices, have existential import. And thus 'there is . . .' need not be depended upon, and worries about its untrustworthiness need not be entertained.

Returning now to our exploratory speculations, there are still misgivings remaining to torment us if we adopt Quine's criterion. For we are depending upon the presupposition that linguistic reference does carry existential import. And this presupposition, natural though it seems, invites, through its very naturalness, further scrutiny. And such scrutiny reveals an interesting fact: there is very little by way of *proof* of the presupposition. Quine's own view relevant to the matter,[11] though charmingly argued, is of no avail here. For he argues that an expression "designates" if and only if existential generalization is valid with respect to it. But if, as we have suggested, the existential quantifier draws its existential force from the presupposition, then we can hardly argue that the presupposition is true because existential generalization is valid with respect to referring expressions. Quine's account, if correct, is rather a mark of "designative" occurrences of expressions than a proof that linguistic reference carries existential import. It is because of the presupposition that existential generalization is valid with respect to certain expressions, rather than that the operation proves the presupposition.

There thus appears to be very little by way of proof of the view that linguistic reference carries existential import. So we are left, it appears, with a genuine *credo*, a substantially unproven, if intuitively plausible, principle upon which criteria of ontological commitment trading upon the supposed existential force of linguistic reference depend. We are committed to the presupposition, and we lack, on the whole, compelling proof of it.

Moreover, there are reasons, perhaps not conclusive, for doubting that linguistic reference does, in fact, carry existential import. There is neither space nor time to explore all of those reasons here, but perhaps a few examples will serve to instill the cold wave of doubt. If we steadfastly refuse to allow ourselves to be obsessed by the indicative mood, such examples seem, at least, readily to appear. The questions 'Is there such a creature as Dracula?' and 'Is it the case that there is a prime number between fourteen and sixteen?' do not provide existential import for 'Dracula' and 'a prime number between fourteen and sixteen'. And the subjunctive mood is likewise instructive: 'If there were such a creature as Dracula, he would enjoy blood sausage'. These sentences are hardly irreferential: we all know what they are supposed to be about. Yet some of their referring expressions do not have existential import. It is obvious that such examples could be multiplied, practically at will. Thus, lacking collateral information, linguistic reference cannot be trusted to have existential import.

These examples have a double disadvantage. First they have a distinctly trivial air about them. Second, they employ moods of discourse which, it might be argued, ought to be exempted from consideration. The case, it might well be argued, ought to be argued on stronger grounds. But the fact is that it can be so argued. There is no need to resort to the interrogative and subjunctive moods. Nor is there any need to resort to 'Dracula' or purported prime numbers. (Indeed, is it not suggestive, given the presupposition, that we can even use such phrases as 'purported prime number' here? The fact is that we do frequently use referring expressions referringly even when there is no referent for them.) The case can be put in terms which are not themselves petty, and which are not subject to petty objections.

The fact is that we can, and often do, refer to what does not exist. And the fact that we do so refer is clearly reflected in the fact that we *would* know what is referred to, *were* it to exist. We make all sorts of references into the past, to entities which are no more. And we make references into the future to entities which are not yet. We talk of Plato, and of the as yet unconceived child to be named 'Plato.' We have, in fact, no reticence at all about referring to what does not exist.

This suggests that we ought to follow and amplify Aristotle by making reference tenseless in order to protect its supposed existential import. We shall have succeeded in referring providing that the intended referent exists, did exist, or will exist, that is, turns out later to exist. Thus our talk of either Plato is referential, though in neither case does there exist a referent at the time when reference is made. And this is good sense: it would surely be nonsense to claim that our present talk about the pupil of Socrates is irreferential.

But it is not at all clear that this strategy will serve to protect the notion that linguistic reference carries (tenselessly) existential import. For there are plenty of cases when we do refer to future events and objects which never come to pass. When the Ladies Club plans its annual picnic, their discussion is not retroactively rendered irreferential just because the picnic is rained out. The same goes for generals planning battles, and such examples could be produced practically endlessly. The same goes for the couple who, wanting a dog, discuss at length the dog they want, even though they never obtain it. And we need not be obsessed with cases involving the intentions of Ladies Clubs or dog lovers. Predictions not involving psychological notions, for example, that the Second Coming will occur in 1984, have the same status: they are not retroactively rendered irreferential by the failure of the events or objects in question to appear on the scene. This is one reason why we must be extremely cautious in supposing that linguistic reference, even in nonfrivolous contexts, always carries existential import. And it ought to make us doubly suspicious of any criterion of ontological commitment which employs that supposition essentially. For linguistic reference, even seriously used, is no sure guide to ontological commitment.

There is obviously much more to be said about reference. For example, the relation between reference and existence has been left largely unexplored, as has the question how to construe denials of existence, and the whole matter of the proper treatment of references which occur within psychological contexts. But all of that must be a tale for another time. Leaving behind these somewhat heretical speculations, it must be pointed out that they leave Quine's criterion pretty much intact, even though they may show that it rests on possibly questionable assumptions. Neither the idea that 'there is . . .' is a necessary mark of commitment (consider 'If there is a battle tomorrow, it will be bloody'), nor the assumption that linguistic reference carries existential import, seems automatically to guarantee Quine's criterion. What might underlie it remains to be seen.

These desultory ramblings hopefully have exposed some suggestions for further inquiry into Quine's criterion. There is no pretense in these pages that Quine's criterion has been conclusively refuted by those ramblings. Rather, the point has been to show that the notion of ontological commitment remains a rich field for philosophical investigation.

Notes

1. See Willard Van Orman Quine, "On What There Is," in *From a Logical Point of View* (Cambridge, Mass.: Harvard University Press, 1953), pp. 1–19.

2. Compare ibid., pp. 102–107. Compare also Quine, *Word and Object* (New York: Technology Press of the Massachusetts Institute of Technology, 1960), pp. 241ff. Quine, *Ontological Relativity* (New York: Columbia University Press, 1969), pp. 66, 93–96, 106. Since I have once already been misunderstood on the point, it should be noted that these three seem to run through the evolving formulations of Quine's criterion.

3. Quine, *Ontological Relativity*, pp. 9–10.

4. Compare "Variables Explained Away," in *Selected Logical Papers* (Random House, 1966), pp. 227–235.

5. "Über die Bausteine der mathematischen Logik," *Mathematische Annalen* 92 (1924).

6. Compare his "On Concept and Object," in *Translations from the Philosophical Writings of Gottlob Frege*, ed. P. T. Geach and Max Black (Oxford: Blackwell's, 1952) pp. 42–55.

7. Everett W. Hall, *What Is Value?* (London, Routledge and Kegan Paul, 1952), chap. 4, esp. pp. 21–34.

8. "Unification of Universes in Set Theory," *Journal of Symbolic Logic* 21, no. 3 (September 1956).

9. "Logic of Many-Sorted Theories," *Journal of Symbolic Logic* 17, no. 2 (June 1952).

10. Note that this is not a case of what Quine calls "substitutional quantification," *Ontological Relativity*, cf. p. 104; rather it is simply to point out that EG and EI are perfectly intelligible even if '($\exists$ x)' is not read "there is."

11. "Designation and Existence," *Journal of Philosophy* 36 (1939).

RESPONSE

Robert Vorsteg

If we accept Quine's criterion of ontological commitment, we thereby bind ourselves to three (further?) commitments: (1) There is *one* channel of ontological commitment; (2) that channel is linguistic reference; and (3) the vehicle of that reference is the bound variable. Dividing his discussion into six sections, Professor Severens notices, in the first three of these, various difficulties or "inconveniences" of Quine's criterion. In the last three he considers whether there might be reasons for rejecting, or at least "shying away from," the criterion itself. Whether or not such considerations entitle us to repudiate Quine's criterion, it is clear enough that Severens regards the three commitments above as poorly founded. In what follows I shall not try to defend Quine or attack him further. I shall simply discuss some of the critical points raised by Severens, with a view to determining their relevance and adequacy as criticisms of Quine's criterion. My purpose is to promote, if possible, a further clarification of the issues involved in the attempt to assess Quine's proposed criterion.

In section 2 Severens points out that Quine's criterion is framed within the context of the logic of quantification, and that this familiar logic can be dispensed with in favor of a logic of combinators. Hence Quine's criterion is relative to the language in which it is framed and "is merely the reflection, *in quantification*, of a more general notion." But if, as Quine contends, the language of quantification is a mere reflection of the ordinary idioms of objective reference, it is not clear how it tells against his criterion to admit that it is thusly relative.

In section 3 we are invited to consider the logical relationship between two tasks: that of formulating a criterion of ontological commitment, and that of determining the ontological commitments of some particular theory or segment of discourse. Severens suggests that we cannot determine a criterion of ontological commitment prior to the recognition of the commitments of at least one theory (or segment of discourse). For how are we to determine, among various linguistic devices, which device is the channel for our ontological commitments, unless we are *already* in a position to recognize the commitments of a given theory? And the mistaken determination of a linguistic device as the ontic channel would yield bogus commitments which we must be in a position to repudiate.

It seems to me correct to say that if we know the ontological commitments of a theory, then, perhaps, we can determine the criterion governing such commitments. But it seems equally correct to say that if we are in prior possession of a criterion, we can determine the commitments of a theory. For it might plausibly be argued: How can we recognize the commitments of a theory unless we are already in possession of some criterion which we invoke either implicitly or explicitly? I do not see that the latter possibility is ruled out by admitting the myriad uses of 'There is . . .' The various examples cited are either clear instances of the nonassertive use of that phrase, or depend upon an appeal to the dubious notion of a *tacit* withholding of the imputation of existence. The prankster could not have his fun unless his auditor understood the utterance 'there is a rattlesnake right behind you' as imputing existence. Surely the prankster intends the remark to be so understood. And what difference is there here between what the speaker intended and what he meant?[1] I suggest that similar considerations apply to 'there is a spy in this room' uttered truly but without knowledge in order to disrupt a meeting.

In section 4 Severens lays down a requirement for any satisfactory criterion of ontological commitment: any such criterion must be neutral with regard to all ontological contenders; it must not rule out any ontological possibilities in advance. Quine's criterion fails here because it rules out Frege's "concepts" and Hall's "facts," for neither of these can be values of bound variables.

To say that Quine's criterion begs the question against, for example, Frege seems like damaging criticism if true. But it seems to me that Quine might readily admit to the question-begging character of his criterion vis-à-vis Frege's concepts and insist that the criterion remains intact, nonetheless. For he may disagree with Severens over the question whether the correctness of Frege's view *is*, after all, beside the point. He might even say (although he need not) that his criterion does not, in fact, exclude concepts "before their case has even been heard." Quine could say that the case for Fregean concepts is a bad case. And, more generally, that a criterion of ontological commitment is none the worse for ruling out bad theories, whether in advance or in retrospect. What would be damaging for the criterion would be the presentation of an ontological contender with impressive credentials of the sort that Quine could not readily show to be spurious. (Cf. Quine's treatment of Wyman's possible entities.) But why should Quine feel compelled to retreat before ontological pretenders?

So long as we can find independent grounds for repudiating putative entities not countenanced by an ontological criterion, I do not see that ontological partiality is an invidious feature of such a criterion.

What about the possibility of alternative criteria of ontological commitment? Quine has insisted that all our ontological commitments are channeled through the referring device of the bound variable. In section 5 Severens notices that some of Quine's own work contains suggestions for an alternative criterion in which the role of the bound variable as the vehicle of reference is depressed in favor of predicates. And a similar result is noticed in the previous work of Wang. These findings would seem to falsify commitments (1) and (3) mentioned above. If so, it then becomes necessary to ask: What is the significance, for Quine's view, of admitting more than one channel of ontological commitment, and admitting that linguistic reference may occur by way of vehicles other than the bound variable? These questions call for comparison of the alternative criteria. We would want to know whether these different criteria yield divergent commitments. If they do not, then the admission of these particular alternatives to Quine's stated criterion would not be disastrous to the program of providing a device determining the ontological commitments of theories. Semantic ascent would still be possible. But if the different criteria do yield divergent commitments, and if the competition between them cannot be rationally resolved in favor of a single criterion, then the point of devising a criterion of ontological commitment would have been lost.

In section 6 Severens invites us to consider two assumptions which might be supposed to guarantee Quine's criterion. These are the idea that 'there is . . .' is a necessary mark of commitment, and the assumption that linguistic reference carries existential import. But neither of these assumptions, we are told, does in fact provide such a guarantee for Quine. The first assumption fails for reasons given by Severens in section 3. I have commented on those reasons and will, accordingly, turn to Severens's remarks concerning the second assumption.

That successful linguistic reference carries existential import is a philosophical commonplace that may be questioned. Severens proceeds to question it and shows, readily enough, that no proof of it is available. More important is his claim that its intuitive plausibility is weakened by the consideration of counterexamples. He cites sentences in the interrogative and subjunctive moods in which the occurrence of referring expressions does not carry existential import. Since he allows that these are problematic cases, I turn to his claim that "we can, and often do, refer to what does not exist." Consider the assertion that the Second Coming will occur in 1984. Severens holds that this assertion is "not retroactively rendered irreferential by the failure of the events or objects in question to appear on the scene." What does it mean to say here that the assertion is not rendered irreferential? It seems to me that an ambiguity lurks in this use of "irreferential." If to refer is to use a referring expression correctly, then, of course, the assertion is not rendered irreferential. But if to refer is, also, to succeed in locating a referent, then, I suggest, the assertion has been rendered irreferential. Hence, although we can refer to what does not exist, the sense in which this is true does not suffice to show that *successful* linguistic reference does not carry existential import.

Note

1. On the relation between what is intended and what is meant by the utterance of linguistic expressions, see John Searle, "What Is a Speech Act?" (especially section 4), in *Philosophy in America*, ed. Max Black (Ithaca, N.Y.: Cornell University Press, 1965), pp. 221–239; and P. F. Strawson, "Intention and Convention in Speech Acts," *Philosophical Review* 73 (October 1964): 439–460.

ADVERBIAL MODIFIERS

Romane Clark

"A curious thing about the ontological problem is its simplicity. It can be put in three Anglo-Saxon monosyllables: 'What is there?' It can be answered, moreover, in a word—'Everything'— and everyone will accept this answer as true." These are the initial three sentences of Professor Quine's essay "On What There Is." [1] "Everything," however, not only answers the ontological question, but remains to be said. For although it is true enough that everything is what there is, it is not true that everything there is exists. There is everything which exists, but more besides. There are, for instance, individuals who did, but do no longer, exist. And species. And calamities which have befallen but passed from us.

Still, there remains ample room for maneuver. It will be objected that it is wrong to say that there are individuals who did, but do no longer, exist. We should say, rather, that there were individuals who existed, but do no longer. We come in this way to see that what there is does, after all, coincide with what exists.

This response, I believe, will not do. The objector will agree that we want to assert not that it used to be that some individuals did earlier, but then came no longer to exist. We wish, rather, to say that it is the case that some individual who did exist does not now. How shall we put this into the blackboard English of logicians? Let us take the 'there are' of the response in the manner naturally suggested, and write 'for some actual'. We might then try this:

1. For some actual individual, x, there is a time, t, earlier than now, and x existed at t but x does not exist now. There is an evident contradiction in equating the actual and the existent in this locational scheme. Shrinking from this, we might instead invoke the modalities of time and, moving the quantifier inside, try this:

2. It was the case that some actual individual, x, existed but x does not exist. But our quasi-English is now ambiguous. It might mean:

2a. It was the case for some actual individual, x, that it was the case that x exists but it is not the case that x exists, or, it might mean:

2b. For some actual individual, x, it was the case that x exists and it is not the case that x exists.

But of course neither of these will do. 2a will not do for it says that in the past it used to be that something existed which does no longer. And 2b, like 1, proscribes on pain of contradiction the equation of what is actual with what exists. But just that was the point of the original protest. (Nor, for that matter, can we then move the quantifier back across the tense modal operator in the following manner:

2c. It was the case that some actual individual, x, exists but x does not exist.

We cannot do this, for the right-hand side of the conjunction must fall within the scope of the quantifier if this is not to be an open sentence. But if it does so, the sentence is then necessarily false.)

So naive first attempts to formulate what we wished to say leave us with the original point. What there is outstrips what exists. There is more to ontology than what there presently is.

We may digress briefly to make a somewhat deeper point. It was parochial anyway to suppose that what there is consists of what the singular referring expressions of a correct theory presently range over. Such a criterion is not after all neutral. It begs the question, for example, against philosophers like Frege (with his unsaturated and unnameable concepts) or Everett Hall (with his unnameable facts, the objects of assertive but not singular reference). Put differently, the criterion presupposes that whatever there is, although not everything there is, can be named. This presupposition can be consistently denied.[2]

For now, we return instead to naive first attempts. These, we remarked, suggest that what there is outstrips what exists. Facing this consequence, we might then try for more sophisticated, and less sophistical, reformulations. We shall not do so here. For I assume that Professor Cocchiarella is right when he argues that "quantification over existing objects, even where such quantification is within the scope of the past tense operator, is not alone sufficient to capture much of what we want to say of past objects."[3] And I assume but shall not attempt to show that there exists a general semantical argument with respect to such a logic to support this point. But assuming all this then, what moral shall we draw?

The moral is this, that we take verbal inflections and verbal modifiers seriously. If "ordinary quantification" reinforced by modal statement operators of tense is insufficient to the task, then we had better try something else which is sufficient. Note that verbal modifiers, appearing in the inflections of the copula or in adverbial modifiers in our native tongue, are quite adequate. Given them, our simple temporal judgments of existence fall out quite neatly. We say in blackboard English with the new resources 'some formerly-existing individual is not presently-existing,' (i.e., perhaps, 'is not identical with any presently-existing individual'). Or more simply, there was an individual who does not now exist. Our quantifiers, with copula now suitably inflected or modified, not merely range over the presently existing inventory, but over past individuals as well.

It has not been common practice to take the inflections and verbal modifiers seriously, much less to do anything serious with them. Common practice has instead shunted modifiers or inflections of the copula off to function as species of classical modal operators. Or the occurrence of predicate modifiers has been cloaked, unremarked, by invoking enlarged numbers of atomic predicates which are opaque with respect to any internal logical complexity. There are difficulties with each of these common practices.

Chaucer had a negation inflection:

> Allas, deth, what ayleth the,
> That thou noldest have taken me,
> Whan thou toke my lady swete,
> That was so fair, so fresh, so fre[4]

Poetry succumbs, with the merest twinge, to logic. "Thou noldest have taken me" goes, apparently, without alteration in truth-conditions, into explicit contemporary prose: 'it is not the case that you would have taken me.' We are tempted to generalize this treatment of syncategorematic modifiers to all verbal modifiers and inflections of the copula. ('Nil,' 'nis,' and 'nam,' in this way become: it is not the case that it will be the case that . . . ; etc.) We have already seen that it is doubtful that tense inflections can be treated in this way. And, generalizing, there is need to be scrupulous in placing our modifiers, now construed as statements operators, with respect to the scope of quantifiers. (For that matter, even homely negation is not immune, as we have learned. 'It is not the case that the present King of France is bald' is ambiguous, leaving us to choose between 'the PKF *nis* bald' and 'the PKF is nonbald'.) Moreover, there are differences between statement operators and modifiers of the copula. For one thing, the former, the *de dicto* modifiers, iterate significantly. The latter, the *de re* modifiers, appear not to. We have, thus, 'it's not the case that it is not the case that John is here,' but not 'John nis nis here'. (That 'it is not the case that John nis here' is significant is another matter.) There are principles for distributing statement operators through the truth-functional compounds they may govern. But the relation between a modified copula and the complex verbal expression it may govern is not so simple. 'This was once a new car' may be thought to entail that this was once new and that this was once a car, but 'Taku was once a Japanese gardener' hardly distributes 'was once' in this way. Taku, if once a Japanese is always a Japanese, as long as he exists. There is, then, need for caution in paraphrasing copula modifiers away in favor of statement operators.

Professor Kenny sharpened the edge of a major difficulty concerning the other group verbal modifiers: the predicate modifiers. It is true, suppose, that Brutus stabbed Caesar, at noon, in the Forum, with a knife. This entails that Brutus stabbed Caesar with a knife. How shall we formalize this valid inference? The premise invokes a predicate, 'stabbed,' of degree five, suitably concatenated with references to agent, patient, time, place and instrument. The conclusion invokes a predicate, again 'stabbed,' but now of degree three, and concatenated only with references to agent, patient, and instrument. We need the resources to express this valid argument, as a valid argument, employing throughout only fixed predicates of constant degree. Let us call the problem of how to do this, Kenny's Problem.[5] Professor Davidson, using only the formal resources of extant, standard, quantification theory, suggests a way to handle Kenny's Problem.[6] It requires, essentially, references to events. Later, we shall have to face Davidson's way with Kenny's Problem, and see what alternatives may be available to us.

For now, however, the point is this: we see that there are formal problems which turn on the presence of verbal modifiers. These formal problems appear, moreover, to have ontological implications. Our task then, is to sort out some of the formal features imposed by the presence of verbal modifiers, and to assess the apparent ontological implications of doing so. In what follows we attempt first a characterization of some of the gross features of any adequate adverbial logic. Appealing to these, we attempt next to meet the conditions of Kenny's Problem. Doing so, we can say something of Davidson's way out and the appeal to events.

I. Adverbial Logic: Some Preliminaries[7]

We distinguish predicate modifiers from predicates. Modifiers cannot, alone, in general be ascribed to subjects. This is marked most clearly with adverbs: 'John is drunkenly' has no standard sense. Modifiers do however attach significantly to predicates. This is not to say that they are predicates of higher type attaching to predicates. Predicates, and so higher type predicates, attach to singular terms and not to predicates. (Piety, not pious, is a virtue.) Rather, predicate modifiers are operators which, attached to a predicate (of degree greater than one), yield a predicate. 'John staggered drunkenly' is all right. Here 'drunkenly' is a modifier which, attached to the predicate 'staggered,' yields an enlarged predicate, 'staggered drunkenly'.

We do not distinguish here inflections and modifiers of the copula from verbal modifiers in general.

Let us call predicates which contain no predicates as parts, "core predicates."

We suppose we are given a stock of core predicates of every type and of varying degree greater than zero. We think of these as bracketed units with carets marking the positions suitable for singular terms: $[P^1(\wedge)], \ldots, [Q^2(\wedge,\wedge)], \ldots$, etc. '$[P^1(\wedge)]$' might be, say, 'is drunk'.

We are already familiar with syncategorematic predicate modifiers. (Usually, but not invariably as we have seen, these are thought to collapse into sentential operators.)

Of the categorematic predicate operators, we have a main division into those which do, and those which do not, yield a predicate of new degree when applied to a predicate. Rather as inserting names into a predicate yields a predicate of lower degree, so modifying a predicate with certain operators may create a new predicate of greater degree. The occurrence of prepositions is often a symptom of this in English.

So we imagine a stock of predicate operators of varying degree also being made available: $[O_i^1(\wedge)], \ldots, [O_m^2(\wedge, \wedge)], \ldots,$ etc.; each enclosed in surrounding brackets, carets again marking the places for individual terms. '$[O_k{}^\circ]$' might for instance be 'slowly'. '$[O_j^1(\wedge)]$' might, for instance, be 'at'. '$[O_j^1$ (midnight)$]^\circ$' would then read 'at midnight'.

We are able now to pile modifiers upon modifiers upon predicates to create complex predicates. Thus, if 'ran' is a core predicate of degree one, say, '$[R^1(\wedge)]$,' then 'ran slowly' is a complex predicate also of degree one which looks like this: $([O_k] [R^1 (\wedge)])^1$. 'Ran slowly at' is a predicate further enriched by the occurrence of the preposition. It is a predicate of degree two, and looks like this: $([O_j^1(\wedge)] ([O_k{}^\circ] [R^1(\wedge)])^1)^2$. Finally, 'John ran slowly at midnight' is a predicate of degree zero, that is, a sentence with the gaps of the previously described predicate filled in order by the singular terms 'midnight' and 'John'.

Evidently, the earlier assertions about Brutus and Caesar differ only in complexity from that about John's nocturnal habits, but not in kind. Before, however, we can come to grips with Kenny's Problem, we require a pair of distinctions in order to set aside certain deviant or irrelevant cases.

The first of the pair of distinctions is fairly straightforward and, for present purposes, can be handled rather summarily. Call predicate modifiers for short "pred-mods." Not all of our verbal modifiers are pred-mods. Some are operators which, when attached to predicates, do not, as do pred-mods, yield new predicates. Instead they yield nonsense. So, these modifiers of modifiers require separate treatment. Call these operators for short "mod-mods." Mod-mods are modifiers which, when attached to pred-mods, yield pred-mods. Sample occurrences of mod-mods are the occurrences of 'very' and 'exquisitely' in the contexts 'very nearly died' and 'exquisitely sensitive performance'. (Here 'very' modifies 'nearly' but not 'died'; 'exquisitely' modifies 'sensitive' but not 'performance' and not 'sensitive performance'. It seems fairly clear that mod-mods can be recursively characterized in an acceptable syntactical fashion and so distinguished from pred-mods and predicates. Since we are concerned only to distinguish them from items with which we later must deal, we can now set mod-mods to one side.

The second distinction among modifiers is in a sense more fundamental and philosophically more interesting. The modifiers divide in a semantical dimension depending upon the way they affect the predicates they come to modify. Some pred-mods create a predicate whose extension is a subclass of that of the predicate modified. 'Red' is one that does so when attached, say, to 'wagon'. Let us think of contexts in which occurrences of pred-mods so function semantically, as "standard." Derivatively, we can think of pred-mods themselves, and complex predicates themselves, as a standard or not. By no means, of course, are all pred-mods standard. And there are within the class of nonstandard pred-mods various distinct species. A rough division is this: there are pred-mods which have a neutralizing effect upon the predicate with which they are concatenated. That is, we cannot tell from the ascription of the enlarged predicate to an object whether the object belongs to the extension of the contained predicate or not. 'Alleged', 'putative', 'seems', and 'possible' are examples of such modifiers. An alleged thief may or may not, in fact, be an actual thief. Let us call these modifiers, "neutralizers."

There are pred-mods the application of which creates a predicate whose extension is necessarily distinct from that of the predicate to which it is applied. 'Fake', 'toy', 'mock', 'nearly', 'almost', and 'simulated' seem to be examples. A toy gun is not a gun but a toy; a fake Cezanne is not a Cezanne although it is a painting; a task nearly done is not done but is only partially done. Let us call these modifiers, "shifters."

There are pred-mods the application of which permits us to infer that an object to which a predicate so modified is ascribed does not belong to the extension of the predicate which came to be modified. 'Fictional', 'imaginary', 'mythological' are examples. A fictional or mythological horse is not a(n actual) horse. Let us call these modifiers, "negators." 'Nis', of course, is our paradigm of an ascription-negating modifier.

Where, then, do the tense modifiers and inflections go: 'formerly', 'once', 'was', and the rest? These create enlarged predicates with extensions necessarily different, but not necessarily distinct, from that of the contained predicate. 'John was,' but perhaps still is, 'lodge president.' Let us call these modifiers, "diversifiers."

These divisions among pred-mods are gross enough, and no doubt incomplete. But they are sufficient to make it clear that some inference conditions must be imposed which depend upon the types of pred-mod which occur in a given sentence.

A perspicuous notation would distinguish pred-mods from mod-mods. The former in turn should be syntactically indexed to display at least the following information: the *level* of the modifer. A modifier of the level $n + 1$ attaches to an expression of level n to create an expression of level n.

The *degree* of the modifier. A modifier of degree n attached to a predicate of degree m yields a predicate of degree $m + n$.

The *kind* of modifier: standard, nonstandard neutralizing, etc. A predicate which results from the application of a given kind of modifier may in turn be indexed as to its kind. Thus the application of a neutralizing modifier to a predicate yields a nonstandard, neutralized predicate. We cannot validly infer from the fact that John may be guilty that he is or that he is not guilty. A cross-classification of the kinds of predicates, standard and nonstandard, with the kinds of modifiers, standard and nonstandard, which can be applied to them, will suggest a pattern of inferences which an adequate adverbial logic should make available. We shall not pause to describe this pattern now.

Finally, the modifiers should carry an indication of their scope. Most are unary operators, applying to predicates one at a time. Some are binary, creating a predicate from a pair of predicates. 'Jane danced or sang all night long.'

The least set of "well-formed modifiers" and "well-formed predicates" could now be recursively characterized. We shall be content with a sample. For example, core predicates are well-formed predicates. And the result of prefixing a unary well-formed modifier of level $n + 1$, degree d, kind: neutralizer, to a predicate of level n, degree e, and kind: negator, yields a predicate of the lower level n, and combined degree $d + e$, which is a neutralized predicate. The qualifier, 'may be', attached to the predicate 'is a fictional teacher at an English girl's school' is an instance of such a predicate, which is true of Miss Jean Brodie.

Although my mind has changed on the issue, it is, I now believe, a serious flaw in the present characterization that it permits the iteration of operators which are identically the same. ('John repaid the loan with a dollar, with a dime' seems not merely false, but nonsense, but the complex predicate it embodies is created quite in accord with the principles briefly mentioned.)

Winking at this, however, it is now possible to return to the Forum. Our problem, i.e., Kenny's Problem, was to characterize the inference which moved from the premise 'Brutus stabbed Caesar, at noon, in the Forum, with a knife' to the simpler consequence, 'Brutus stabbed Caesar with a knife'. We need to characterize this inference in a manner which preserves the validity of the inference but employs no predicate which changes its degree in its various occurrences in the space of the argument.

2. Kenny's Problem Examined: Davidson's Way Out

Davidson, we remarked, offers an analysis of this problem which appeals to nothing richer in logical resources than standard, first-order logic. Evidently, if the analysis is otherwise acceptable, we shall want to take Davidson's way out. We need to characterize briefly this approach.

It was Davidson's belief that action sentences at least do not display their true logical form in their grammatical form. We commonly think, for example, that "Shem kicked Shaun" is a simple sentence consisting of two names and a two-place predicate. It was Davidson's suggestion however that such sentences "should be construed as containing a place, for singular terms or variables, that they do not appear to." In particular, it was his suggestion in this instance "that we think of 'kicked' as a three-place predicate." We write, thus: $(\exists x)$ (Kicked(Shem, Shaun, x)). And we read: "There is an (event), x, such that x is a kicking of Shaun by Shem." [8]

Ordinary logic, plus references to events, turns out to be sufficient for Kenny's Problem. 'Brutus stabbed Caesar, at noon, in the Forum, with a knife' is now seen to be a grammatically disguised assertion whose logical form is more clearly displayed thus: There is an (event), x, such that x is a stabbing of Caesar by Brutus, and x is a noon-event, and a Forum event, and a knife event. English to one side, this existential assertion has the important logical merit that its truth guarantees the truth of the simpler sentence, the sentence that Brutus stabbed Caesar with a knife. It does this, moreover, invoking throughout constant predicates of fixed degree. The conclusion, read in Davidson's event-prose, reads this way: There is an (event), x, which is a stabbing of Caesar by Brutus and is a knife event. 'Stabbing' remains in the conclusion what it was in the premise, a two-termed relation. Davidson's analysis meets the requirements of Kenny's problem.

It is clear that Kenny's problem is quite general, reaching beyond sentences which employ verbs of action. It is equally clear that Davidson's solution is also quite capable of generalization. The problem is a formal one which is not unique to the concept of action. It occurs whenever we move inferentially from a sentence containing a richly modified predicate to one otherwise the same but with the predicate less richly modified. For example, we have reports, not only of actions, but of the states, offices, and natures of things. Jones perhaps, was staggering drunk, from wine, in his room, at 10 o'clock in the morning. Smith, perhaps, is an alumni trustee, of Duke, in Durham, for a two-year term, beginning now. It follows from the former that Jones was drunk in the morning. It follows from the latter that Smith is a trustee of Duke. Davidson's way with action sentences provides a schema for the analysis of these simple inferences. We can restore the validity of these simple inferences and employ only predicates of fixed degree in doing so—provided merely that we can come up with the appropriate types of suppressed singular terms. But these are always, in cookbook fashion, available. These can always be created by forming a verbal noun phrase from a given sentence. Thus, to 'John is dumb' we have 'John's being dumb'. And now we can quantify to heart's content, for 'John is dumb' may be viewed as grammatically misleading, disguising its true logical nature. Logically, we may say: There is a (state), x, such that x is John's being dumb. And there is, then, as well the state: Jones being drunk. And the office: Smith's being a trustee.

There are a number of difficulties, I believe, with Davidson's way out. Some turn upon fairly fussy logical points; for instance, some are points which concern how neutralizing, and shifting, pred-mods function on his analysis. And some are points which concern the formulation in event-prose of adverbs of manner, like 'slowly,' and some concern the semantics of his event ontology. But these issues can be suppressed here. For the overriding, pointed, difficulty, which directly touches the concerns of this conference, lies in Davidson's rain-forest ontology. His solution, generalized as we see it can (and believe it must) be, commits us to ineliminable references to events, states, and offices and the like. Since his solution meets the requirements of Kenny's Problem, our task can be put this way: is it possible to analyze sentences with predicate modifiers in such a way that the analysis satisfies the two parts of Kenny's Problem but does so without invoking references to events, states, and the like?

3. Kenny's Problem Examined: The Role of Adverbial Modifiers

The answer, I believe, is "yes." We have seen that it is possible to display the internal complexity of predicates as a function of their modifiers. So it remains to specify some of the inferential relationships which predicate modifiers appear to impose upon the sentences in which they occur. It is our hope to achieve with an enriched formal structure, but reduced ontology, what Davidson achieved with a standard formal structure but inflated ontology.

Consider a string of touching pred-mods of the same level and kind. Stacked pred-mods meeting this description may be permuted without description. This approximates to a certain use of commas in piling up modifiers in English. If Brutus stabbed Caesar, at noon, in the Forum, with a knife, then Brutus stabbed Caesar with a knife, in the Forum, at noon.

The positioning, and hence the scope, of nonstandard modifiers is a matter of some delicacy when formalizing natural statements. But where this is formalized unambiguously, the general principle of permutation for modifiers is assumed still to apply, even within complex predicates themselves governed by some nonstandard pred-mod. Thus, 'Tom seems to be an intelligent, sensitive boy' has, we claim, matching truth-conditions to 'Tom seems to be a sensitive, intelligent boy'. Permutation of the touching, standard pred-mods, 'intelligent' and 'sensitive', remains even within the scope of the neutralizer, 'seems'.

Let us call the principle governing such operations with touching modifiers of the same kind, the Permutation Principle.

An *initial segment* of a predicate is a core predicate or the result of prefixing a modifying operator to an initial segment. We can now lay down some detachment principles for predicates.

Any standard predicate implies any initial segment of itself (the Detachment Principle).

We understand predicate implication in this way, that to say that one predicate, P, implies another, Q, is equivalent to saying that the statements, P*, and Q*, which result from uniformly replacing the individual term positions associated with the various occurrences of the same core predicates and same modifiers by singular terms, are such that P* implies Q*.

It follows from the characterization above that if it is true that Brutus stabbed Caesar at noon, in the Forum, with a knife, then it is also true that Brutus stabbed Caesar with a knife, in the Forum, at noon. This, by the Permutation Principle for modifiers. And it follows from this last as well, that Brutus stabbed Caesar with a knife. This, by the Detachment Principle for modifiers, for the predicate of this last is an initial segment of that of the premise.

It will be noted that although piling up modifiers may result in the creation of new predicates of increased degree, no one predicate changes its degree in any of its occurrences. Throughout the inference, from richly modified characterization of that ancient assassination, to the reduced, implied segment of the original, 'stabbed' remains a predicate of degree two.

So it is that we meet the minimal requirements imposed by Kenny's Problem as these are illustrated by the simple example which employed only standard predicates throughout. And we do so, if our sketch of a theory of adverbial modifiers is good in full detail, without making special appeals to special entities: to events, states, offices, facts or the like. This is not to say, of course, that core predicates may not carry places for references to events or states. It is merely to say that we are not forced to construe them as doing so by sheer logical considerations; not, at least, by Kenny's Problem. Our metaphysics must make its own way.

It remains to generalize the account a bit. Not all contexts will involve only standard predicates and standard pred-mods, yet Kenny's Problem may well apply to some of these.

The Detachment Principle for standard predicates can be extended to cases where a standard initial segment occurs as part of some larger, not necessarily standard predicate. Thus:

If '. . . P' is a predicate in which P occurs as a standard initial segment, then if P implies Q by the Detachment Principle for modifiers, '. . . P' implies '. . . Q' (Contextual Detachment).

This holds for segments embedded in neutralizing, shifting, or diversifying, predicate contexts. It does not hold, however, for occurrences within the scope of negators. Thus, from 'Brutus apparently stabbed Caesar, at noon, in the Forum, with a knife' we may infer that Brutus apparently stabbed Caesar with a knife. (These sentences, of course, must be distinguished from that which asserts that Brutus stabbed Caesar, apparently at noon, . . . etc.) We cannot, however, infer from the assertion that Brutus did not stab Caesar, at noon, etc., that Brutus did not stab Caesar with a knife.

Neutralizing and diversifying pred-mods sanction no further inferences, affirmative or negative, with respect to the predicates they may modify. From the fact that an agent may be, or was once, an F nothing follows as to his presently being so. But negators and shifters do sanction a further inference. From their occurrence we may infer the negation of the predicate which they modify. They differ in themselves in that we cannot validly generalize existentially over the former, but may do so with the latter. From the fact that my child's toy is a model truck it follows that there is something actual which is a model truck but not a truck. But if 'Bolay' is the name of my child's imaginary playmate, we correctly conclude that Bolay is not a playmate of my child, but surely not that Bolay actually exists.

It will perhaps have been noticed that none of the principles which have been cited justifies the detachment of attributive adjectives from the predicate complexes in which they may occur. We cannot, on the strength of just these principles, infer, for instance, that the bug before me is large, or that it is red, from the fact that the bug is a large, red, chigger. This may seem untoward. But what we can infer, via our principles, is that it is a large chigger, and that it is a red one. And despite appearances all this, I think, is as it should be. For the creature may be large for a chigger, but tiny for an insect. We may say, roughly, that things are not large or small in themselves, but rather are so only relative to some class or kind of things. This, it seems, extends to all adjectives which take comparatives. For, while one might complain that 'red' after all seems to stand alone on its own feet in a way 'large' does not, it is not merely logical simplicity that suggests lumping these different adjectives together. This may be a very red chigger, but not be, after all, very red.

We have now accumulated a certain set of intuitions concerning, and inferential principles governing, adverbial modifiers. Evidently, these scattered intuitions and piecemeal principles cry for the support of an articulate semantical structure in which to express the truth-conditions for the correct application of modifiers to predicates.[9] But, postponing that fundamental task, it is fairly clear, I think, that our main, negative conclusion remains: we are not forced by Kenny's Problem to embrace an ontology of events. Moreover, there are some interesting suggestions as well that emerge. We conclude with just one of these. It is appropriate to terminate our discussion, as we began, with Quine. Quine wrote: "Perhaps I can evoke the appropriate sense of bewilderment as follows. Mathematicians may conceivably be said to be necessarily rational and not necessarily two-legged; and cyclists necessarily two-legged and not necessarily rational. But what of an individual who counts among his eccentricities both mathematics and cycling? Is this concrete individual necessarily rational and contingently two-legged or vice-versa?" [10]

'Necessarily', 'contingently', 'possibly', the modalities *de re*, belong among our adverbial modifiers. So an adequate adverbial logic should not stand tongue-tied, toes inward, before Quine's challenge. 'Is, as such' and 'is-*qua*' are also adverbial modifiers and are available to us. Shall we say that John, our cycling mathematician, is essentially rational? Or shall we say instead that he is as such, i.e., is-*qua* mathematician, so? And that he is as such, i.e., is-*qua* cyclist, not so? Perhaps. What it would mean to say these things is an interesting further question for a theory of modifiers.[11]

Notes

1. Willard Van Orman Quine, "On What There Is," in *From a Logical Point of View* (Cambridge, Mass.: Harvard University Press, 1953), pp. 1–19.

2. See Romane Clark, "Facts," *Southern Journal of Philosophy* 4, (Fall 1966): 123–136. This was an attempt to examine Hall's tacit denial of the presupposition concerning nameables and the existent.

3. Nino B. Cocchiarella, "Existence Entailing Attributes, Modes of Copulation and Modes of Being in Second Order Logic," *Nous* 3 (1969): 33–48.

4. *The Book of the Duchess*, ll. 481–484.

5. Anthony Kenny, *Action, Emotion, and Will* (London: Routledge and Kegan Paul, 1963), pp. 156–162.

6. Donald Davidson, "The Logical Form of Action Sentences," in *The Logic of Decision and Action*, ed. Nicholas Rescher (University of Pittsburgh Press, 1967), pp. 81–120.

7. This section draws heavily on two sources. I borrow directly from an earlier, unpublished paper of mine, "In Any Event: Davidson's Analysis of the Logical Form of Action Sentences." The account is in various ways flawed and incomplete, but still seems to me essentially correct. This paper was first presented at Indiana University in December 1968.

I am particularly indebted to the second source, the exciting, unpublished paper of Terence D. Parsons, "A Semantics for English," especially Part I. He, of course, bears no responsibility for what I do here. But many things for which I was groping fell into place, and I could excise some mistakes in my attempts, after reading his paper. The appeal to predicate modifiers was common both to his paper and my attempts to develop the Indiana address. He had a much more developed system, and finer discriminations among modifiers which alter the extensions of predicates which they modify, than had occurred to me.

8. Davidson, *The Logic of Decision*, p. 92.

9. The principles suggested here match only in part those suggested by Parsons in "A Semantics for English." The natural semantics for these seems to me closer to the notions described in Adam Morton, "Extensional and Non-truth-functional Contexts," *Journal of Philosophy* 66 (March 27, 1969): 159–164, than to that developed by Parsons.

10. Willard Van Orman Quine, *Word and Object* (Cambridge, Mass.: Technology Press of the Massachusetts Institute of Technology, 1960), p. 199.

11. Professor Georg H. von Wright's dyadic logics seem natural vehicles to attempt to exploit in working out an answer. See, e.g., his "An Essay in Deontic Logic and the General Theory of Action," *Acta Philosophica Fennica*, fasc. 21 (Amsterdam: North-Holland, 1968).

RESPONSE

Scott A. Kleiner

Professor Clark is concerned with two problems in his provocative paper. The first is that standard first-order predicate logic with modal operators for past (and future) tenses is not sufficiently rich for stating that an object once existed but no longer exists. The second is that the formal analysis of certain arguments in standard first-order predicate logic, for example, Kenny's argument and the like, presupposes recipes allowing one to cook up without restriction a seemingly unlimited variety of ontological *species,* for example, events, states, offices, facts. According to Professor Clark, both problems can be resolved by introducing predicate modifiers and accompanying syntax, semantics, and rules of inference.

My concern here will be with the first problem, that of providing a formal language capable of describing things in the past that no longer exist. Rather than commenting directly upon Professor Clark's proposals, I would like to explore some of their ramifications vis-à-vis natural science. We will see that the special theory of relativity (STR) has ontological import that seriously threatens the metaphysical utility Professor Clark attributes to his predicate modifiers. Yet these expressions may well find their place in resolving certain semantic puzzles that arise regarding scientific theories dealing with the past.

The very acceptance of this first problem carries a kind of ontological commitment, viz. that advanced by Professor Clark in the first paragraph of his paper: "For although it is true enough that everything is what there is, it is not true that everything there is exists. There is everything which exists, but more besides. There are, for instance, individuals who did, but do no longer exist." Professor Clark would probably also agree that there are individuals that will but do not now exist.

One could conceivably adopt alternative ontological beliefs of this kind. "There are objects that will but do not now exist and all objects that did exist still exist," expresses one such alternative. Another alternative can be stated thus: "All objects that will exist exist now and all objects that did exist still exist." If either one of these claims, or some other claim contradicting Professor Clark's ontology, can be justified, Professor Clark's problem is a pseudoproblem and can be dismissed.

In what follows I will consider an argument advanced by Hilary Putnam[1] to the effect that STR entails the existence of at least one object in the future. The argument is easily extended to support the claim that there exists at least one object in the past. And we can even push Putnam's argument one step further to show that all past and future objects exist. This last claim contradicts Professor Clark's ontology, and hence it appears that the first part of his enterprise is not consistent with STR.

Putnam's argument is somewhat redundant and in places obscure, but I hope that the simplified version I give here will make his point without distortion.

A fundamental postulate in the theory of relativity is that the set of material reference-frames is nonempty. That is, at any time in which the theory is applied at least one material reference frame exists. It is with respect to such a frame that an origin for space-time coordinates can be specified. An inertial frame must be a material object with mass and must be capable of velocities less than the speed of light. A spatial point cannot be in motion and a massless material object (e.g., a photon) cannot move less than the speed of light. This first postulate can be instantiated and expressed informally as follows:

1. Reference frame Oxt exists.

As STR has had many successful applications to systems containing more than one moving material object, we can plausibly make a second assumption

2. Reference frame $Ox't'$, distinct from Oxt, exists.

Let us consider a case, some application of STR, that meets these further conditions:

3. The origin of reference frame $Ox't'$ coincides in space with Oxt's origin at some initial moment t_o, and it moves along the x-axis with a velocity v near to but not equal to the velocity of light, c. (This assumption is expressed in terms of quantities t_o and v defined in Oxt.)

4. Suppose that a is a momentary time-slice of Oxt at t_o, i.e., a is a point on Oxt's world-line and a has the date t_o.

5. Suppose also that b is a momentary time-slice of $Ox't'$ occurring at t_o in Oxt and at t_o' in $Ox't'$.

It is easy to show that the simultaneity of spatially coincident events is invariant under Lorentz transformation. That is, if two spatially coincident events are simultaneous in one inertial reference frame, they are simultaneous in all such reference frames. Hence a and b can be dated either at t_o or t_o'.

Most physical and cosmological theories formulated within the framework of STR assume the existence of a number of other objects at varying distances from the origins of whatever reference frames used. Thus the following assumption should not make our case atypical:

6. At t_o' in $Ox't'$ there exists some thing c, where c is a momentary time-slice of an object located at x_1' in $Ox't'$.

Assumption 6 may be the weakest link in the argument, and perhaps a little more should be said in its defense. We have assumed that there can exist time-slices with which we can have no communication. We are notified of its existence only after the time-slice has become past, and on some views, notice comes only after the time-slice has ceased to exist. This delay is a consequence of the law ascribing a finite velocity to light, another principle fundamental to STR.

One might be tempted to reject the existence of objects from which we can receive no signals, thus rejecting assumption 6. Rejecting 6 and holding Professor Clark's ontological position is tantamount to claiming that each object in the universe exists for itself (and for whatever else might share its position) and for that object no other object located at a different position exists. This position has been termed *pluralistic solipsism*,[2] and since we have no grounds for assuming that there is or can be an observer on every reference frame, it is a materialistic and not a subjectivistic solipsism.

Now it seems to me absurd to claim that material objects exist for anything, especially for other noncognitive material objects. The only sense of 'exists for' that has any currency is that in 'celestial spheres exist for Aristotle,' i.e.,'Aristotle believes that celestial spheres exist.' However neither Professor Clark's essay, my comments, nor the STR are concerned with beliefs. I see nothing to be gained by introducing a new relation 'exists for' to be borne by pairs of material objects.

I would now like to introduce a relation R to be borne by a pair of momentary objects if and only if both objects exist. The relation R can be viewed as a refinement of the ordinary relation of coexistence. Just as the student of physical geometry and motion (the kinematicist) refines the commonplace relation 'position' so that it holds between two pointlike material objects, the relation coexistence can be refined to hold between two momentary time-slices of a material object. Our final assumption is that R is an equivalence-relation.

7. The relation of coexistence, R, is reflexive, symmetrical and transitive.

The reflexivity of R is an immediate consequence of the law of identity (for all x, x is identical to x). The case for R's symmetry and transitivity is less conclusive than is the case for reflexivity.

However it does seem obvious to me that a coexists with b if and only if b coexists with a. It seems equally obvious that if a and b coexist, then if b and c coexist then a and c coexist (assuming, of course, that a, b, and c are all momentary objects).

Now let us return to the Lorentz transformations. In $Ox't'$, b and c occur simultaneously, i.e., both occur at t_o'. But b and c are at different locations; b is at x_o' and c is at x_1'. It follows by the Lorentz transformations that in Oxt the times for b and c, say t_b and t_c, are different, i.e.,

$$t_b = \gamma(t_o' + vx_o'/c^2)$$
$$t_c = \gamma(t_o' + vx_1'/c^2)$$

where x_o' and x_1' are the respective positions of b and c in $Ox't'$. Subtracting these equations gives

$$(t_c - t_b) = (v\gamma/c^2)(x_1' - x_o').$$

Accordingly, if $x_1' > x_o'$ (if c occurs to the right of the origin in $Ox't'$) then $t_c > t_b$, i.e., event c occurs later than event b from the viewpoint of Oxt. Since a and b coexist (assumptions 4 and 5) and b and c coexist (assumptions 5 and 6), a and c coexist (assumption 8), that is, a exists if and only if c exists. Hence at least one future event, viz. c, exists. A similar argument with the assumption that $x_1' < x_o'$ shows that at least one past event exists.

Finally, by choosing the appropriate values for v, the argument can be extended to an event occurring at any time whatever in Oxt. As v approaches c, the quantity $v\gamma/c^2$ approaches infinity. Hence we can make $t_c - t_b$ as large as we please simply by choosing a sufficiently large relative velocity for our two frames, Oxt and $Ox't'$. We can thus prove the existence of any event whatever, no matter how distant it is in the past or the future. All events that ever existed exist, and all events that will exist exist.

We are apparently driven to a form of determinism wherein, e.g., future sea fights already exist and hence an admiral's decisions are predetermined. Perhaps the conclusions of this argument will be less discomforting if we recall that STR, like classical particle mechanics, classical continuum mechanics and classical electrodynamics, is deterministic in another sense as well. That is, the direction and curvature of each material world-line, (the velocity and acceleration of each material particle) is uniquely determined by its initial position and direction and the forces to which the object is subject at any momentary stage.

We know now that not all physical theories are deterministic in this second sense. Positions and velocities cannot be so uniquely determined in quantum mechanics. The success of quantum theories has shown that classical Newtonian and relativistic theories are limited in their applicability.

Classical Newtonian and relativistic theories are applicable only in cases in which both initial position and velocity as well as applied forces are well-defined and known. Position and velocity in the classical sense are not simultaneously well-defined in the quantum domain (Heisenberg's uncertainty principle).

We do not at present know to what extent classical mechanical quantities, perhaps supplemented with classical electromagnetic and thermodynamic quantities, will be helpful in predicting and retrodicting past and future developments in biological evolution or in human affairs. More specifically, we do not know what part quantum as opposed to classical behavior plays in these processes, and we do not know all of the forces to which such processes are subject at various stages. Also, such processes may be governed by quantities and interactions distinct from those now in use in physics.

In STR the future events that are predetermined by their existence are presumed to be fully described in classical terms, terms that are not adequate for describing events and processes in the quantum domain. In this domain we must use probability distributions *(stochastic quantities)* such as Schrödinger's Ψ-function for probable position. A relativistic theory expressed in these latter terms does not entail the existence of determinate future events. Rather, if we follow Popper[4] and Feyerabend,[5] we need suppose only the existence of certain *dispositions* described by the probability distributions.

Thus, if stochastic quantities such as those used in quantum mechanics are necessary for the description of evolutionary processes or events brought about by human actions, STR does not entail that the future outcome of such processes and such events now exist. At worst, STR entails only the existence of dispositions whereby one rather than another outcome is more or even equally likely.

Accordingly, we need take seriously the classical STR's ontological implications only where that theory is known to be applicable. In fields such as evolutionary biology, social, political, and economic history, we might provisionally adopt Professor Clark's ontology. There, at least provisionally, we might accept as legitimate his problem of describing in formal terms past objects that exist no more.

My final remark is that I think that Professor Clark's adverbial modifiers, in particular his diversifiers, may be of considerable importance in illuminating methodological guidelines embedded in historical theories, i.e., theories that appear in the fields of geology (geogeny), biology (biogeny), and perhaps social, political, and cultural history.

For example, in evolutionary biology we would say that the predicates 'is a reptile' and 'is a former reptile' carry different methodological import and hence differ in their meaning. The investigator should expect to apply the former predicate to objects that are now to be found alive in various locations around the world or that are now capable of biting or of other reptile behavior. However, the latter predicate applies only to objects that once were and are not now capable of such behavior. Evidence that 'is a former reptile' applies will include traces of reptilian fossils but not bites or anatomical features of live animals.

On the other hand, the two predicates share a common core of methodological import. Skeletal and other past and present anatomical characteristics are relevant to classifying past and present animals as reptiles. Although the meanings of these predicates differ they remain linked via this common core.

Accordingly, I offer the suggestion that the common methodological and semantical characteristics of the predicates given above can be associated with the core predicate 'is a reptile'. The modifier 'former' or perhaps better 'former (vertebrate)' then has associated with it some of the observational and experimental methods differentiating the paleontologist's from the field biologist's investigations.

Notes

1. Hilary Putnam, "Time and Physical Geometry," *Journal of Philosophy* 64 (1967): 240–247.

2. Howard Stein, "On Einstein-Minkowski Space-Time," *Journal of Philosophy* 65 (1969): 5–23.

3. K. R. Popper, "Quantum Mechanics without 'The Observer,' " in *Quantum Theory and Reality*, ed. M. Bunge (Berlin: Springer-Verlag, 1967), pp. 7–44.

4. P. K. Feyerabend, "Problems of Microphysics," in *Frontiers of Science and Philosophy*, ed. R. G. Colodny (Pittsburgh: University of Pittsburgh Press, 1962), pp. 189–283.

GOD, MODALITY, AND ONTOLOGICAL COMMITMENT

Bowman L. Clarke

The problems of the existence of God, modality, and ontological commitment have historically been brought together in those arguments traditionally called ontological arguments. The purpose of this essay is to investigate these problems from the perspective of these arguments by raising this question: Under what conditions is one committed to accepting as true the sentence, 'It is necessary that God exists'? Following Carnap,[1] however, I want to distinguish between two different questions, one an internal question and the other an external question. The internal question concerns what a particular theory commits one to, and the external question concerns one's commitment to a particular theory. With this distinction in mind, we can divide our original question into two questions. The first, or internal question, is: Under what conditions does a particular theory commit one to accepting as true the sentence 'It is necessary that God exists'? The second, or external question, is: Under what conditions is one committed to a particular theory in which the sentence 'It is necessary that God exists' is true? These are two quite different questions and must be answered on quite different grounds.

I

In order to treat this first question I want to analyze two historical arguments, which we will call Leibniz's Ontological Proof and Findlay's Ontological Disproof, within a theoretical context. Leibniz's argument, which is found in the *Monadology*, runs as follows:

A. God alone . . . has this prerogative, that he must exist if he is possible.

B. And since nothing can hinder the possibility of that which possesses no limitation, no negation and consequently no contradiction,

C. this alone is sufficient to establish the existence of God a priori.[2]

In order to treat this argument within a theoretical context, let us assume a hypothetical theory which consists of a set of individuals, the domain of discourse, and a set of sentences about these individuals and governed by the classical rules of sentential logic. Among these sentences, let us assume one in particular, 'God exists', which we will at present simply abbreviate, '*G*'. In order to incorporate modality into our hypothetical theory, let us add a monadic sentential operator, '*P*', which will be read, 'It is possible that . . .', along with the following definitions:

MD 1. '*Np*' for '$\sim P \sim p$'

MD 2. '*Cp*' for '*Pp* · *P* $\sim p$'

MD 3. '*Ip*' for '$\sim Pp$'

'*Np*' will be read, 'It is necessary that *p*'; '*Cp*' will be read, 'It is contingent that *p*'; and '*Ip*' will be read, 'It is impossible that *p*'. Fortunately at this point we do not have to assume any modal axioms, nor, as a matter of fact, even the rules of quantification. Since our hypothetical theory is intended to be about God, let us call this hypothetical theory, theory T.

Sentence A of Leibniz's argument can safely be translated into theory T as follows:

1.1 *PG ⊃ NG*.

And by "translate" here, and elsewhere in this paper, I mean no more than that if we accept Leibniz's premise A then we would want premise 1.1 as true in theory T. It should also be pointed out that premise 1.1 is, by *MD* 1 and *MD* 2, logically equivalent to the sentence, '$\sim CG$', or 'It is not the case that it is contingent that God exists'. Following Charles Hartshorne,[3] let us refer to this premise as Anselm's Principle.

Sentence B of Leibniz's argument is somewhat more complicated, for it is an elliptical subargument. We might spell it out in this fashion:

D. Nothing can hinder the possibility of the existence of an individual whose concept does not imply a contradiction.

E. The concept of an individual which contains no limitation and no negation cannot imply a contradiction.

F. The concept of God contains no limitation and no negation.

G. Therefore, nothing can hinder the possibility of the existence of God.

For the present purposes, we shall consider only the conclusion of this subargument, which we can safely translate into theory T as follows:

1.2 PG.

Premise 1.1 and premise 1.2, by Modus Ponens, logically imply:

1.3 NG,

which would be the translation of Leibniz's conclusion, sentence C, into our theory T.

Before we consider further the premises of the proof, 1.1–1.3, let us consider, alongside this proof, Findlay's Ontological Disproof. Findlay accepts, it would seem, Leibniz's first premise, for of the existence of God, he writes: "There must be no conceivable alternative to an existence properly termed 'divine': God must be wholly inescapable . . . whether for thought or reality." [4] It would certainly appear safe to translate this into our theory as '$\sim CG$', which as we have seen, is logically equivalent to

2.1 $PG \supset NG$.

The second step in Findlay's argument is to deny in the name of "all who share a contemporary outlook" [5] the sentence 'It is necessary that God exists'. Thus, the second premise of Findlay's argument might be translated into theory T as '$\sim NG$'. This, however, by MD 1 and double negation is logically equivalent to '$P \sim G$'. So for purposes of comparison, let us take as the translation of Findlay's second premise,

2.2 $P \sim G$.

From 2.1 by MD 1, we get

2.3 $PG \supset \sim P \sim G$.

And from 2.2, by double negation, we get

2.4 $\sim \sim P \sim G$.

From 2.3 and 2.4 by Modus Tollens we get

2.5 $\sim PG$,

which is, by MD 3, logically equivalent to:

2.6 IG.

Thus Findlay appears right: "Plainly, (for all who share a contemporary outlook) . . . the Divine Existence is either senseless or impossible." [6] Since we, under our operating assumptions, took 'G' to be a well formed sentence of theory T, if we accepted both 2.1 and 2.2, the only alternative for us would be to accept "the Divine Existence" as impossible.

I have set up these two arguments, 1.1–1.3 and 2.1–2.6, in this way to dramatize several logical points: (1) The only difference between Leibniz's Ontological Proof and Findlay's Ontological Disproof, as translated, is the difference between the two second premises. (2) If we accept Anselm's Principle in theory T and at the same time accept both 'PG' and '$P{\sim}G$', the two second premises, then theory T will be contradictory. In fact, Anselm's Principle, which as we saw is logically equivalent to '${\sim}CG$', is, according to MD 2, simply the denial of '$PG \cdot P{\sim}G$'. (3) If theory T is not to be inconsistent, then we must either deny Anselm's Principle, or find some way of justifying the choice of 'PG' over '$P{\sim}G$'. If we are to salvage theory T from inconsistency, then best we explore the justifications that have been given for all three of these premises.

First, let us take what we have called Anselm's Principle. If the "God-is-dead" theologians of recent vintage have evidence for their claim, then of course we would want to reject Anselm's Principle in theory T. But due to the lack of evidence, as well as clarity, in their writings, perhaps we should take the principle more seriously. After all, the metaphor of God as creator, one of the more basic religious metaphors, is certainly an attempt to picture God as necessary for the existence of any other individual; if he didn't exist then nothing would exist. If we included in our hypothetical theory T sentences asserting the existence of a number of individuals; then if it could be truly said of a particular individual, 'It is possible that it exists and it is possible that it does not exist', then surely this individual would hardly qualify as the individual called God in Western religious tradition. Here, I think, Findlay[7] is right; such an individual might deserve the veneration due the saints, but hardly the worship due to God. If we want theory T to be about the individual traditionally called God, then we need to hold on to Anselm's Principle as long as we can and examine the justifications that can be given for accepting the two premises 1.2 and 2.2 as true in theory T.

Let us examine, then, the justification which Leibniz gives for the premise, 'PG'. In the analysis of the subargument, we saw that his justification rests upon a consistent conception of God and the general principle: Nothing can hinder the possibility of the existence of an individual whose concept does not imply a contradiction. In order to consider adding such a general principle to theory T, we will have to assume that we have added to theory

T the classical rules of quantification theory. And if, in this context, we think of Leibniz's 'concept' in terms of a descriptive definition, we could translate this general principle in terms of the following rule:

Rule A. Given any definiens, 'Dx', for some definiendum, 'Qx', if 'Dx' is not contradictory, then '$P(\exists x)Qx$' is true. With rule A added to theory T, then if we can formulate a consistent definition for the expression, 'x is God,' which we will abbreviate 'Gx', then theory T commits us to accepting '$P(\exists x)Gx$' as true. And this, in conjunction with Anselm's Principle, commits us to accepting '$N(\exists x)Gx$' as true. And on the surface of things, there appears to be no reason for not accepting rule A as a part of theory T. Before, however, we give the prize to Leibniz, let us examine the justifications which have been offered for what we have translated as Findlay's premise 2.2, '$P\sim(\exists x)Gx$'.

Here, however, we do not want to commit ourselves to "a contemporary outlook" unless we know exactly what that is and how it is to be justified. According to Findlay[8] this "contemporary outlook" is the outcome of the Kantian criticism of the Ontological Proof. Findlay, no doubt attempting to avoid chauvinism, does not mention Hume; but Hume, perhaps as much as Kant, is responsible for this "contemporary outlook," which Findlay has in mind. So let us see how Hume and Kant would justify our accepting as true, the premise, '$P\sim G$', or the logically equivalent one, '$\sim NG$'.

For a look at Hume's justification, I want to take an argument presented by Cleanthes in the *Dialogues Concerning Natural Religion*. The argument is offered as an attempt to demonstrate that the existence of God is not demonstrable. This is to be accomplished by first demonstrating the more general principle: The existence of no individual is demonstrable. The argument runs as follows:

A. Nothing is demonstrable unless the contrary implies a contradiction.

B. Nothing that is distinctly conceivable implies a contradiction.

C. Whatever we conceive as existent, we can conceive as nonexistent.

D. There is no being, therefore, whose nonexistence implies a contradiction.

E. Consequently, there is no being whose existence is demonstrable.[9]

If Cleanthes' argument is sound, then we would surely want to take '$P \sim (\exists x) Gx$' as true in theory T. Consequently we can view this argument as an attempt to justify Findlay's premise 2.2. When we examine Cleanthes' argument carefully, we find, however, that it is a rather strange argument. Cleanthes seems to think that premises B and C imply D, and that premises D and A, in turn, imply the conclusion, E. But this is not the case. B and C together imply instead,

D'. If the existence of a being is conceivable, then its non-existence does not imply a contradiction.

Then D' and A together will imply a quite different conclusion,

E'. If the existence of a being is conceivable, then the existence of that being is not demonstrable.

Thus what appears to be a justification for the premise '$P \sim (\exists x) Gx$', is instead a justification for the premise,

3.1 $P(\exists x) Gx \supset P \sim (\exists x) Gx$.

But this would follow directly from Cleanthes' premise C. Thus it appears that Cleanthes' argument is either invalid or circular. And the crucial premise C remains unjustified.

Before, however, we offer an alternative suggestion for Cleanthes, let us examine what Findlay himself takes as a justification for his premise 2.2; that is, Kant's criticism of Descartes' Ontological Proof. Let us consider as two premises the following two statements from the *Critique of Pure Reason*:

A. I cannot form the least concept of a thing which should it be rejected with all its predicates leaves behind a contradiction.

B. In the absence of contradiction, I have . . . no criterion of impossibility.[10]

From these two premises, Kant appears to want to get the following conclusion:

C. There is nothing the nonexistence of which is impossible. If Kant can reach C, then of course he will have offered for us justification for accepting premise 2.2, '$P \sim (\exists x) Gx$'. So let us see how Kant argues from A and B to C. What he obviously needs is an additional premise such as the following:

D. If the rejection of the concept of a thing does not leave behind a contradiction, then the rejection of the existence of that thing does not leave behind a contradiction.

D in conjunction with A and B would then yield C.

Unlike Cleanthes, Kant has introduced in his argument a distinction between "the concept of a thing" and "the existence of a thing." His justification for D is his famous argument which is too often superficially summarized as, "existence is not a predicate." What Kant wants to argue, however, is that existence is not a determining predicate, only a logical predicate, and as such, it neither adds to nor subtracts from the conception of a thing. Therefore, what is true of the concept of a thing (i.e., its negation does not imply a contradiction) will likewise be true of the existence of the thing; consequently premise D.

In order to treat Kant's argument as carefully and accurately as possible, let us again make use of the quantifiers. Also, for purposes of bringing the argument up to date, let us think in terms of a 'definition of a thing' rather than a 'concept of a thing'. To do this, we shall have to introduce a schema for definitions such as,

D1. 'Qx' for 'Dx',

where 'Dx' is the definiens for some definiendum, 'Qx'. Kant's first step is as follows:

E. If, in an identical proposition, I reject the predicate while retaining the subject, contradiction results.[11]

Interpreting "identity" here in terms of logical equivalence, Kant is telling us that according to D1, then the following is logically true,

4.1 $Qx \equiv Dx$.

Granted this equivalence, if we assert 'Qa' and deny 'Da' then we will have a contradiction, and of course he is right. In contrast, he points out,

F. But if we reject subject and predicate alike, there is no contradiction; for nothing is left that can be contradicted.[12]

Thus, if we deny both 'Qa' and 'Da' then no contradiction will result. Here again Kant is right, provided 'Dx' is not tautologous; for from 4.1 itself, we can get the logical equivalence,

4.2 $\sim Qx \equiv \sim Dx$.

Kant then makes this crucial move:

G. If existence is rejected, we reject the thing with all its predicates; and no question of contradiction can arise.[13] In short, Kant seems to be advocating, as analogous to 4.2, the following logical equivalence,

4.3 $\sim (\exists x) Qx \equiv \sim Dx$.

That this equivalence is what Kant is proposing can be substantiated in three ways. First, it fits the analogous discussion centering around 4.1 and 4.2. Secondly, it jibes with what he says in the particular case of God: ". . . if we say 'There is no God', neither omnipotence nor any other of its predicates is given, they are one and all rejected together with the subject. . . ." [14] Thirdly, it is precisely what he needs to justify the critical premise D.

This logical equivalence in theory T, however, would be disastrous, particularly when we realize that 'Dx' could be any consistent definiens which we care to introduce into the theory, and consequently, any consistent sentence matrix. From D1 we could always get

4.4 $\sim(\exists x)Dx \equiv \sim Dx$,

which analogously to 4.1, with double negation, yields

4.5 $(\exists x)Dx \equiv Dx$,

for any sentence matrix we might choose for a definiens. '$Dx \supset (\exists x)Dx$' is an acceptable logical theorem of quantification theory, but '$(\exists x)Dx \supset Dx$' is disastrous. Existence may be a logical predicate rather than a determining predicate, but this cannot be interpreted as asserting 4.3 as a logical truth. Yet this is precisely what Kant needs in his argument; otherwise he has no justification for premise D.

I have analyzed the arguments of Cleanthes and Kant, not so much as an effort to point out their weaknesses, but as an effort to find what is needed to justify premise 2.2 as true in our hypothetical theory T. And this, I think, has emerged clear. It is a rule analogous to Leibniz's rule A and which could be stated something like this:

Rule B. Given any definiens, 'Dx', for some definiendum, 'Qx', if 'Dx' is not tautologous (i.e., '$\sim Dx$' is not contradictory), then '$P\sim(\exists x)Qx$' is true.

If rule B were accepted as a part of theory T, then we could prove a translation of Cleanthes' critical premise, '$P(\exists x)Qx \supset P\sim(\exists x)Qx$'. Likewise, this rule would function analogously to Kant's critical premise D, and then we could prove Findlay's premise 2.2, '$P\sim(\exists x)Gx$'.

Assuming a consistent and nontautologous definiens for the expression, 'x is God' (and any other would be useless), then we can conclude: (1) theory T, with Anselm's Principle and rule A, commits us to accept as true the sentence, 'It is necessary that God exists'. (2) theory T, with Anselm's Principle and rule B, commits us to accept as true the sentence, 'It is impossible that God exists'. (3) theory T, with Anselm's Principle and both rule A and rule B, is inconsistent. (4) There appears intuitively to be no reason for choosing rule A and rejecting rule B, or for choosing rule B and rejecting rule A.

These facts, I think, clarify why many philosophers have so strongly defended the Ontological Proof, while others, equally as strongly, have attacked it. This, I would propose, is the modern theistic modal paradox. In the absence of any clear reason for choosing rule A and rejecting rule B, or for choosing rule B and rejecting rule A, there appear to be only two ways out of this paradox: Either reject Anselm's Principle or find some good reason for rejecting both rule A and rule B. The first alternative is an uninteresting one for a theological reason. The theological reason is that given by Findlay and mentioned earlier: To reject the principle is to give up the theological task as it is traditionally conceived. This leads us to explore the possibility of some reason for rejecting both rule A and rule B as rules for theory T. But the choice of this alternative also necessitates our finding some alternative to rule A for justifying premise 1.2, '$P(\exists x)Gx$', in theory T.

2

The only reason I know for rejecting a rule, which might intuitively appear acceptable, is that the following of the rule has consequences which we would not want to accept. When Russell was able to demonstrate that the following of Frege's rule for forming classes produced a contradication, then Frege was willing to give up his rule despite the fact that it had appeared, intuitively, to be quite acceptable. In a similar vein, I hope to show that rule A and rule B taken as a part of a particular theory will have consequences which I do not think that we would find acceptable.

In order to do this I want us to consider another hypothetical theory, which we will call theory CI. Theory CI will be an interpreted calculus of individuals, in the Goodman and Leonard[15] sense of the term. It does not matter, however, what we take to be the domain of discourse, we only assume that there is one. We will also assume, again, the classical rules of quantification theory, along with the modal machinery of theory T, and rule A and B. Theory CI will, in addition, have one primitive two-place predicate, 'overlaps', which will be abbreviated, 'O', and one axiom governing this predicate,

A1. $(x)Ox,x.$

In theory CI, let us propose two definitions,

D1. 'NOx' for '$\sim Ox,x$'

D2. 'SOx' for 'Ox,x'.

The first definition is the definition for a "nonoverlapping," and the second for a "self-overlapping individual." With rule A as a part of theory CI, we are committed to accepting as true in theory CI the following sentence,

5.1 $P(\exists x)NOx,$

since the definiens, '$\sim Ox,x$' is not self-contradictory. Likewise, with rule B as a part of Theory CI, we are committed to accepting as true the following sentence,

5.2 $P\sim(\exists x)SOx,$

since 'Ox,x' the definiens, is not tautologous. Now, according to D1, 5.1 yields

5.3 $P(\exists x)\sim Ox,x;$

and, according to D2, 5.2 yields

5.4 $P\sim(\exists x)Ox,x.$

If we compare 5.3 with A1, we find that theory CI has committed us to asserting as true something rather strange. Sentence 5.3, by quantification theory, is logically equivalent to

5.5 $P\sim(x)Ox,x.$

Thus theory CI commits us to asserting that every individual in the domain of discourse overlaps itself and, at the same time, commits us to asserting that it is possible that at least one individual in the domain of discourse does not overlap itself. Strictly speaking, of course, A1 and 5.5 are not contradictories. If, however, we accept '$(x)Ox,x$' as an axiom delimiting the domain of discourse for theory CI, then it would seem natural to accept as true in the theory, the following sentence,

5.6 $N(x)Ox,x.$

But 5.6 is, according to MD 1, logically equivalent to

5.7 $\sim P\sim(x)Ox,x,$

which is the contradictory of 5.5.

The situation with 5.4 and A1 is analogous. For A1, by quantification theory, yields

5.8 $(\exists x)Ox,x$.

Now it seems strange for theory CI to commit us to saying that there is one individual that overlaps itself and, at the same time, to commit us to saying that it is possible that there is no such individual. Strictly speaking, here again, 5.8 and 5.4 are not contradictories in theory CI. But having assumed that the domain of discourse of theory CI is not empty, it would seem natural to want to accept as true in theory CI, the following,

5.9 $N(\exists x)Ox,x$.

And this sentence, by MD 1, is logically equivalent to

6.1 $\sim P \sim (\exists x)Ox,x$,

which is the contradictory of 5.4.

In the light of these facts, it appears that rule A and rule B should be replaced in theory CI with a rule such as the following, where 'S' might be any sentence of theory CI:

Rule C. 'PS' is true if, and only if, it is not the case that 'S' in conjunction with axioms, '$A_1 \ldots A_n$' logically implies a contradiction.[16]

With rule C, then theory CI commits us to accepting as true 5.6, '$N(x)Ox,x$', and 5.9, '$N(\exists x)Ox,x$'. For since '$\sim (x)Ox,x$', in conjunction with Al, logically implies a contradiction, then '$P \sim (x)Ox,x$' is false and '$\sim P \sim (x)Ox,x$' is true. Likewise, since '$\sim (\exists x)Ox,x$', in conjunction with A1, logically implies a contradiction, then '$P \sim (\exists x)Ox,x$' is false and '$\sim P \sim (\exists x)Ox,x$' is true. Consequently, theory CI would commit us to rejecting both 5.3 and 5.4 as false. What rule C does, in fact, is map, in terms of the modalities, the consequences of Quine's criterion of ontological commitment, "To be is . . . to be the value of a variable," [17] into the object language of the theory. For according to Al, theory CI countenances as values for variables only what D2 defines as "self-overlapping individuals." This, in effect, is asserted by 5.6. And according to Quine's criterion, theory CI necessarily commits us to the existence of those kinds of individuals. This, in effect, is asserted by 5.9.

Russell, Whitehead, and Peirce have often criticized philosophers of the modern period on the grounds that they could not treat relations adequately with their logical machinery, and consequently, could not take relations seriously. The difficulties of rule A and rule B, in contrast with rule C, can be interpreted as evidence for the criticisms by these three philosophers. The difficulty with rule A and rule B is that they do not take relations seriously. Any theory which includes primitive relations, which do not appear trivially in the theory, requires axioms governing these relations. And it is this fact that is not taken into account by rule A and rule B.

Let us now return to our hypothetical theory, theory T. Given rule C as a part of our theory, let us raise the question of the justification of premise 1.2 in the Leibniz Ontological Proof, that is, 'It is possible that God exists'. Here I want to follow a suggestion made by Charles Hartshorne. His attempt to justify premise 1.2 is quite different from Leibniz's attempt, that is, rule A. In the *Logic of Perfection*, for example, Hartshorne writes of this premise: "The postulate of logical possibility . . . is in my view the hardest to justify. One way of doing this is to employ one or more of the theistic proofs, some forms of which demonstrate that perfection must at least be possible." [18] It is this suggestion, that the other proofs might be used to justify premise 1.2, that I wish to explore. In order to do this, let us examine St. Thomas's first of his Five Ways.[19] In this analysis we shall not be interested in either the validity or the soundness of the proof, only in the logical machinery used in the formulation of the proof. The proof may conveniently be summarized as follows:

A. Some things are in motion.

B. Whatever is in motion is moved by something.

C. Nothing moves itself.

D. Therefore, whatever is in motion is moved by another.

E. In any series of movers and things moved, subsequent movers are moved only in so far as they are moved by the first mover of the series.

F. No series of movers and things moved can go on infinitely; that is, have no first movers, or final member of the series.

G. Therefore, it is necessary to arrive at a first mover, moved by no other.

H. And this everyone understands to be God.

I would like to propose that in this proof, St. Thomas has made use of the following:

1. A relation and the field of that relation: In this case, 'x moves y'; or what he in the *Summa Contra Gentiles* calls an "ordered series of movers and things moved." [20]

2. A definite description locating a unique individual in the

field of that relation, or what Carnap in *The Logical Structure of the World*[21] calls a structural definite description: In this case, "the first mover, moved by no other."

3. An assertion that the field is not empty: In this case, A.

4. A series of sentences giving the formal properties of that relation, what Carnap[22] would call a structural description: In this case, the relation is irreflexive (B, C, D), transitive (E) and has a first member (F).

5. An assertion that the existence of the first unmoved mover necessarily follows from the structural description: In this case, G.

6. A sentence maintaining that the term, 'God', names the individual located by the structural definite description: In this case, H.

For our purposes, this one analysis is sufficient, but it might be pointed out in passing that the Second, Third and Fourth Ways make use of precisely the same logical machinery. In the Second we have the relation, 'x is the efficient cause of y', its field and the structural definite description, 'the first efficient cause'; in the Third, 'x is contingent upon y', and 'the first which is contingent upon no other'; in the Fourth, 'x is better, or more noble than y', and 'the best, or most noble'. What is even more interesting, from a historical viewpoint, is that the so-called ontological argument of St. Anselm in the *Proslogium*[23] makes use of precisely the same logical machinery. Here, however, St. Anselm is concerned with an order based on the relation, 'x is greater than y', and the structural definite description in this case is, 'that than which nothing greater can be conceived', or 'the greatest', which, according to him, even the fool understands to be God.

We are now in a position, I think, to state the conditions under which theory T, with rule C, would commit us to accepting as true the sentence, 'It is necessary that God exists'. They are as follows:

1. That theory T have a set of primitive relations, '$R_1 \ldots R_n$' and a set of consistent axioms, '$A_1 \ldots A_n$' governing these relations.

2. That theory T have a consistent structural definite description, '$(\exists x)Dx$', for the constant, 'God'.

3. That the sentence, '$\sim(\exists x)x = $ God', in conjunction with axioms, '$A_1 \ldots A_n$', logically imply a contradiction.

Under these three conditions, theory T would commit us to accepting as true both of the following:

7.1 $P(\exists x)x = \text{God}$
7.2 $N(\exists x)x = \text{God}$

For according to condition 3, '$(\exists x)x = \text{God}$' in conjunction with the axioms would not logically imply a contradiction, and, by rule C, '$P(\exists x)x = \text{God}$' is true. Likewise according to condition 3, '$\sim(\exists x)x = \text{God}$' in conjunction with the axioms does logically imply a contradiction, so '$P\sim(\exists x)x = \text{God}$' is not true and '$\sim P\sim(\exists x)x = \text{God}$' is true. Also, from this sentence, by addition, we can get,

7.3 $\sim P(\exists x)x = \text{God } v \sim P\sim(\exists x)x = \text{God}$,

which is, by the rules of sentential logic and MD 1, logically equivalent to

7.4 $P(\exists x)x = \text{God} \supset N(\exists x)x = \text{God}$,

Anselm's Principle. Thus under these three conditions Anselm's Principle itself is derivable, which is as it should be.

3

Having isolated the conditions under which theory T would commit us to accepting as true the sentence, 'It is necessary that God exists'; let us assume that theory T does in fact meet these conditions, in order that we might raise our second question: Under what conditions is one committed to a particular theory in which the sentence, 'It is necessary that God exists', is true? This second question, unfortunately, is a far more difficult one to answer than the first. Perhaps, however, we might get some insight into an answer if we consider some possible objections one might give to accepting theory T.

These objections, I think, would be of three different kinds: (1) One might wish to question one or more of the logical rules and axioms (including the modal ones) of theory T, as, for example, Quine has questioned modal logic in general:

> ... the way to do quantified modal logic, if at all, is to accept Aristotelian essentialism. ... Such a philosophy is as unreasonable by my lights as it is by Carnap's or Lewis's. And in conclusion I say, as Carnap and Lewis have not: so much the worse for unquantified modal logic as well; for, if we do not propose to quantify across the necessity operator, the use of

that operator ceases to have any clear advantage over merely quoting a sentence and saying that it is analytic.[24]

(2) One might question the structural definite description for the term, 'God', in theory T, as, for example, St. Thomas questions the structural definite description given by St. Anselm: "Perhaps not everyone who hears this name *God* understands it to signify something than which nothing greater can be thought, seeing that some have believed God to be a body." [25] (3) One might wish to reject one or more of the descriptive axioms, '$A_1 \ldots A_n$,' of theory T, as, for example, Whitehead rejects those of St. Thomas's First Way: "Today we repudiate the Aristotelian physics and the Aristotelian cosmology, so that the exact form of the . . . argument manifestly fails." [26]

All three of these possible objections to theory T are refusals to accept a certain rule or rules of the theory. We could, along analogous lines, answer our second question by simply saying that one is committed to theory T if he accepts the rules of theory T. But this answer is obviously a trivial one; it reduces the question of commitment to a theory to no more than a biographical or historical question. The fact that Quine finds quantified modal logic "unreasonable by his lights," or as he puts it later, "uncongenial to him," [27] is for those interested in Quine, an interesting fact of Quine's biography. Likewise, the fact that someone else finds quantified modal logic, on the other hand, to be reasonable by his lights and quite congenial to him, would be no more than perhaps an interesting fact of that person's biography. The fact that some have not understood the name 'God' to signify something than which nothing greater can be thought and believed God to be a body may be an important fact for an ancient historian, just as the fact that we today repudiate the Aristotelian physics and the Aristotelian cosmology is, for us, a rather important fact about contemporary culture. Analogously, the fact that some person or persons accepted the structural definite description in theory T for the constant, 'God', or accepted the descriptive axioms, '$A_1 \ldots A_n$,' of theory T would be no more than an interesting biographical or historical fact about that person or persons. Surely more than a biographical or historical fact is expected as an answer to our question concerning the conditions under which one is committed to theory T.

What we generally want as an answer to our second question is, I think, something quite different. We want to know. Under what conditions *should* one be committed to a particular theory, for example, theory T? We want an evaluation of the theory itself. And it is around this question that most philosophic controversy rages. Yet I know of no better general answer to this question of the evaluation of a theory than that given by Carnap. In speaking of a linguistic framework, or what in this paper we might refer to as the framework of a theory, he writes: "It can only be judged as being more or less expedient, fruitful, conducive to the aim for which the language is intended." [28] In short, a theory is a tool, it serves a purpose; and the condition under which a person should be committed to a particular theory is that that theory be the most efficient tool available for accomplishing that purpose.

The difficulty with this answer, however, is that we are seldom clear about the purposes of our theories, and this is particularly true of theology today. In fact, there does not even exist a theory T which meets the conditions which we have outlined. This may, of course, be due to the fact that we do not know yet how to construct such a theory; but I would think that it is more likely due to the fact that we are not yet clear as to what purpose such a theory would serve. Also, we are a long way from having clearly formulated criteria for evaluating one theory as more or less efficient than another in accomplishing some given purpose. These two facts taken together, the lack of clarity of purposes and the lack of clear criteria for evaluating theories, are probably the greatest single factor contributing to philosophic controversy. We are not likely, however, to have either, clarity of purposes or clear criteria for evaluating theories, until a great deal more work is done in the area of theory construction. But until we are somewhat clearer about these matters, we, as philosophers, would perhaps do well to take seriously Carnap's principle of tolerance, extending it even to theology, and to heed his warning: "To decree dogmatic prohibitions of certain linguistic forms . . . may obstruct scientific progress." [29]

Notes

1. Rudolph Carnap, *Meaning and Necessity* (Chicago: University of Chicago Press, 1956), pp. 206–208.

2. G. W. Leibniz, *Selections*, ed. Philip P. Wiener (New York: Scribner's, 1951), pp. 541–542.

3. See Charles Hartshorne, *The Logic of Perfection* (LaSalle, Illinois: Open Court, 1962), p. 51. Strictly speaking the above formulation is not the formulation which Hartshorne uses for Anselm's Principle. He uses the formula, '$G \supset NG$', and derives '$PG \supset NG$' by using Becker's Postulate. '$G \supset NG$' is not, however, a faithful rendering of Hartshorne's own statement of the principle: ". . . perfection could not exist contingently." This statement translated into theory T would be ' $\sim CG$', which is logically equivalent to '$PG \supset NG$,' not '$G \supset NG$.' Using our formulation of the Principle, the need for Becker's Postulate in Hartshorne's proof is eliminated.

4. J. N. Findlay, "Can God's Existence be Disproved," *New Essays in Philosophical Theology*, ed. Antony Flew and Alasdair MacIntyre (London: SCM Press, 1958), p. 52.

5. Ibid., p. 54.

6. Ibid.

7. Ibid., p. 53.

8. Ibid., p. 54.

9. David Hume, *Dialogues Concerning Natural Religion*, ed. Henry D. Aiken (New York: Hafner, 1948), p. 58.

10. Immanuel Kant, *Critique of Pure Reason*, trans. Norman Kemp Smith (London: Macmillan, 1963), p. 503.

11. Ibid., p. 502.

12. Ibid.

13. Ibid.

14. Ibid.

15. Henry S. Leonard and Nelson Goodman, "The Calculus of Individuals and Its Uses," *The Journal of Symbolic Logic 5* (June 1940): 45–55.

16. Here rule C is not necessarily proposed as a primitive rule, nor are we concerned here with any particular modal axioms. All that is intended here is that it be a rule of the theory, either primitive or derived.

17. Willard Van Orman Quine, "On What There Is," *The Review of Metaphysics* 2 (September 1948): 32.

18. Hartshorne, p. 52.

19. St. Thomas Aquinas, *Summa Theologica*, I, Q. 2, A. 3. All quotations are from *Introduction to Saint Thomas Aquinas*, ed. Anton C. Pegis (New York: Modern Library, 1948).

20. St. Thomas Aquinas, *Summa Contra Gentiles*, I, Ch. 13, 14. Quotation from Anton C. Pegis, trans. *On the Truth of the Catholic Faith* (New York: Doubleday 1955).

21. Rudolph Carnap, *The Logical Structure of the World*, trans. Rolf A. George (Berkeley: University of California Press, 1969), pp. 24–28.

22. Ibid., pp. 21–24.

23. St. Anselm, *Proslogium, Monologium, etc., trans.* S. N. Deane (LaSalle, Illinois: Open Court, 1958), pp. 7–9.

24. Willard Van Orman Quine, *From a Logical Point of View* (New York: Harper and Row, 1963), p. 156. Since we do not have the modal rules and axioms of theory T, we do not know whether or not it allows

for quantification across the necessity operator; however, even if this is not the case, the second half of Quine's criticism would still be applicable.

25. St. Thomas Aquinas, *Summa Theologica*, I, Q. 2, A. 1.

26. Alfred North Whitehead, *Science and the Modern World* (New York: New American Library, 1960), pp. 156–157.

27. Willard Van Orman Quine, "Reply to Professor Marcus," *Contemporary Readings in Logical Theory*, ed. I. M. Copi and J. A. Gould (New York: Macmillan, 1967), p. 299.

28. Rudolph Carnap, *Meaning and Necessity*, p. 214.

29. Ibid., p. 221.

RESPONSE

John Heintz

I

In his paper, Professor Clarke attempts to give a satisfactory solution to the "Modern Theistic Modal Paradox." [1] The paradox derives from the inconsistency of three propositions: (1) It is possible that God exists. (*PG*) (2) It is possible that God does not exist. (*P~G*) (3) "God alone . . . has this prerogative, that he must exist if he is possible." [2] This last, a premise in Leibniz's Ontological Proof is symbolized by Clarke as '*PG ⊃ NG*', and christened "Anselm's Principle." [3] Since Clarke defines '*Np*' as '*~P~p*',[4] the consequent of proposition (3), '*NG*', is an abbreviation for '*~P~G*', which is the contradictory of (2). Truth-functional inference yields '*~PG*', the contradictory of (1). Thus (1)-(3) together entail both that it is possible that God exists and that it is impossible that God exists.

Clarke wishes to preserve Anselm's Principle, (3), as an essential part of the characterization of God. He therefore seeks a means for accepting proposition (1) and rejecting proposition (2). The means he settles on include moving from considering God's existence as an isolated question, to treating God's existence as but one of a number of propositions asserted within a theory. The support for each individual proposition will follow from the support one has for the theory as a whole. In general, the possibility of God's existence (1), Anselm's Principle (3), and God's necessary existence will all be consequences of a theory which meets three conditions and contains one rule (primitive or derived) for introducing modalities:[5]

I. That theory T have a set of primitive relations, '$R_1 \ldots R_n$' and a set of consistent axioms, '$A_1 \ldots A_n$' governing these relations.

II. That theory T have a consistent structural definite description, '$(\imath x)Dx$', for the constant 'God'.

III. That the sentence, '$\sim(\exists x)x = \text{God}$', in conjunction with the axioms, '$A_1 \ldots A_n$' logically imply a contradiction.

Rule C. 'PS' is true if, and only if, it is not the case that 'S' in conjunction with axioms '$A_1 \ldots A_n$' logically implies a contradiction.

Rule C, together with II, ensures that the proposition that it is possible that God does not exist, is not a theorem of the theory: that God does not exist is inconsistent with the axioms, by III, and that inconsistency renders '$P \sim G$', 'it is possible that God does not exist,' false by rule C.[6] If '$P \sim G$' is false, its negation, '$\sim P \sim G$', or 'NG', is true, making the necessary existence of God a consequence of the theory. And since 'NG' is true, truth-functional inference guarantees the truth of Anselm's Principle, '$PG \supset NG$'. Clarke's theories embrace (1) and (3) and the negation of (2).

2

Unfortunately, rule C proves too much. Professor Clarke develops his rule in the context of Goodman and Leonard's calculus of individuals.[7] It is an axiom of that theory that each individual overlaps itself:

A1. $(x)Ox,x$.[8]

A1 implies that something overlaps itself: '$(\exists x)Ox,x$'. Therefore, '$\sim(\exists x)Ox,x$', in conjunction with the axioms, implies a contradiction, yielding, by rule C, '$\sim P \sim (\exists x)Ox,x$', 'it is not possible that nothing overlaps itself,' that is, 'it is necessary that something overlaps itself'. As in the case of a theological theory meeting Clarke's conditions, the calculus of individuals, with rule C, guarantees that if it is possible that something overlaps itself it is necessary that something overlaps itself. I do not think that even Goodman and Leonard would have wanted to claim that anyone who understood the concept of an individual would see that if it were possible for something to overlap itself it would be necessary that something overlap itself. The kind of necessity guaranteed by rule C is not any sort of logical or conceptual necessity, but a kind of theoretical necessity of the sort we have in mind in saying such things as 'It is necessary for a man to have oxygen in order to live,'' or, with Professor Severens in an earlier discussion in this conference, that it is not biologically possible to secure a cross between a Saint Bernard and a Chihuahua. Anselm, it seems to me, expected more than this of the concept of God; he expected that anyone who fully understood that concept would understand that if it were possible to satisfy it, it was necessary. One need not be a Christian, and accept Christian theology, to understand that.

Anselmian exegesis aside, it is clear that rule C guarantees the truth of Anselm's Principle for any existential proposition that is part of a theory we accept. It therefore guarantees necessary existence to all those things we may posit in the theories which, in addition to our theology, we employ to understand the world, including set theory arithmetic, physics and chemistry. This guarantee flatly contradicts Leibniz's premise with which we began: "God *alone* . . . has this prerogative, that he must exist if he is possible."

3

Why does Professor Clarke seek to fund the modal questions surrounding God's existence in a theory with rule C? There are good reasons for believing that questions about God should, in general, be set in a theoretical context; Paul Ziff, for one, has explored them in "About 'God'." [9] But Clarke's reasons are not Ziff's. Clarke wants, rather, to make intelligible a context in which it makes good sense to accept his (1), 'It is possible that God exists' but reject (2), 'It is possible that God does not exist'. He finds a reason for accepting (1) in

Rule A. Given any definiens, 'Dx', for some definiendum, 'Qx', if 'Dx' is not contradictory, then '$P(\exists x)Qx$' is true. [10]

The sense of possibility given in rule A comes close to logical possibility and would avoid the sort of objections I have made to rule C modalities. Clarke's problem is that he can see no reason for accepting rule A and rejecting the analogous rule B: [11]

Rule B. Given any definiens, 'Dx', for some definiendum, 'Qx', if 'Dx' is not tautologous (i.e., '$\sim Dx$' is not contradictory), then '$P \sim (\exists x) Qx$' is true.[12]

Just as Rule A generates 'It is possible that God exists,' so rule B generates 'It is possible that God does not exist,' and with it the Modern Theistic Modal Paradox. Professor Clarke comes close to rejecting rule B in his discussion of arguments from Hume and Kant, but he turns away at the last moment.[13] I would like to spend a few moments on this section of Clarke's paper to show why he need not turn away, and to see what difference rejecting rule B might make.

Clarke quotes Kant: "I cannot form the least concept of a thing which should it be rejected with all its predicates leaves behind a contradiction. In the absence of contradiction, I have . . . no criterion of impossibility." [14] Clarke then draws the conclusion for Kant that there is nothing the nonexistence of which is impossible. Clarke complains that Kant's premises do not imply his conclusion, for there is a missing link between the rejection of the concept in the first premise and the rejection of existence in the conclusion. This complaint is based on reading 'concept' as the antecedent for the word 'it' in the premise, which ignores the fact that in German, the word for 'concept' (*Begriff*) is masculine, and the pronoun translated 'it' (*es*) is neuter, corresponding to the German word for 'thing' (*Ding*).[15] Kant is saying that there is no concept of a thing which, should the thing (the existence of a thing corresponding to the concept) be rejected would result in a contradiction. So there is no missing premise which needs to go from rejecting the concept to rejecting the existence of the thing. However, we can ask for Kant's justification of the premise, and this Clarke proceeds to do by examining an argument he quotes in three steps:

E. If, in an identical proposition, I reject the predicate while retaining the subject, contradiction results.

F. But if we reject subject and predicate alike, there is no contradiction.

G. If existence is rejected, we reject the thing and all its predicates; and no question of contradiction can arise.[16]

Clarke then proposes to read "definition" for "concept" and asks to consider a definition

D1. 'Qx' for 'Dx' [17]

and its consequence, that

4.1 $Qx \equiv Dx$[18]

is logically true.

"Granted this equivalence," Clarke says, "if we assert 'Qa' and deny 'Da' then we will have a contradiction, and of course he [Kant] is right" [in asserting E].[19] Then, commenting on F, Clarke says, "Thus, if we deny both 'Qa' and 'Da' then no contradiction will result. Here again Kant is right, provided 'Dx' is not tautologous; for from 4.1 itself, we can get the logical equivalence

4.2 $\sim Qx \equiv \sim Dx$."[20] Clarke seems to be thinking that 4.2 amounts to denying both 'Qa' and 'Da', but of course it is not. 4.2 may be true if both 'Qa' and 'Da' are true: Granted D1, 4.2 will be true whether 'Dx' is tautologous or not. What would not be true, and what would indeed amount to denying both 'Qa' and 'Da' would be the conjunction of their denials:

$\sim Qa$ & $\sim Da$

as Clarke's prose suggests. I have labored this point, because Clarke treats Kant, in G, as advocating the biconditional

4.3 $\sim (\exists x)Qx \equiv \sim Dx$[21]

At most, following Clarke's own reading, rejecting the existence, *and* rejecting the thing with all its predicates would look something like this:

$\sim (\exists x)Qx$ & $\sim Da$.

Unlike 4.3, this is not a biconditional that is sometimes false, it is a denial that anything is Q, and in particular that a is Q. The important fact about the conjunction and 4.3 alike is that they are, in form, contingent rather than contradictory. Clarke says: "Existence may be a logical predicate rather than a determining predicate, but this cannot be interpreted as asserting 4.3 as a logical truth. Yet this is precisely what Kant needs in his argument." [22] Here I am at a loss, for Kant only claims that from rejecting the existence of a thing no contradiction can arise, and 4.3, if that were (which it is not) what Kant intends by a rejection of existence, is not contradictory.

4

Rule B. Given any definiens, 'Dx', for some definiendum, 'Qx', if 'Dx' is not tautologous (i.e., '$\sim Dx$' is not contradictory), then '$P\sim (\exists x)Qx$' is true.[23]

If 'P' represents logical possibility rule B is just false. Let 'Dx' be spelled out as '$Fx \lor \sim (\exists x)Fx$'. Thus spelled out, '$Dx$' is not tautologous, for, for some choices of '*F*' and '*x*', it will come out false; for example, if '*F*' means 'is an astronaut' and the free occurrence of '*x*' refers to Raquel Welch, then '*Dx*' is false, for it is false that she is an astronaut, and it is false that no one is an astronaut. Yet

$$(\exists x)(Fx \lor \sim (\exists x)Fx)$$

is a theorem of logic, and its negation, equivalent to

$$\sim (\exists x)Dx$$

is therefore inconsistent. So despite Kant's arguments about concepts, there are definitions which are not tautologies, but which none the less *must* be satisfied. Rule B is therefore not precisely analogous to rule A, for if '*Dx*' is not contradictory, then neither is '$(\exists x)Dx$'. Argument: If '$(\exists x)Dx$' is contradictory, then by quantifier interchange, '$(x)\sim Dx$' is necessarily true, in which case each of its instances, including '$\sim Dx$' is necessarily true, making '*Dx*' contradictory.

The argument that '$(\exists x)$ $(Fx \lor \sim (\exists x)Fx)$' is necessarily true, however, reveals why it gives little consolation to theists. Suppose 'is a Supreme Being' were defined as '$Fx \lor \sim (\exists x)Fx$'. Then '$(\exists x)$ $(Fx \lor \sim (\exists x)Fx)$' would be true whether anything were *F* or not. For if nothing were *F*, the following argument would work:

$\sim (\exists x)Fx$	Hypothesis that nothing is *F*
$Fx \lor \sim (\exists x)Fx$	By addition and commuting the disjunction
$(\exists x)$ $(Fx \lor \sim (\exists x) Fx)$	By existential generalization.

Again, if nothing were *F*, then everything would be God!

$\sim (\exists x)Fx$	Hypothesis that nothing is *F*
$Fa \lor \sim (\exists x)Fx$	By addition and commuting the disjunction

The above argument goes for any constant '*a*'. Only Spinoza could be pleased to discover that everything is God.

Including a uniqueness condition in '*F*' will not help. If '*Fa*' happens to be true, for some individual constant '*a*', then indeed '*Fb*' would be false for any individual constant '*b*' that referred to something different from what '*a*' referred to. But '$(\exists x)$ $(Fx \lor \sim (\exists x)Fx)$' can be true if there is nothing which meets condition *F* by being the unique thing possessing the properties delimited in '*F*'. Thus Professor Clarke may, and indeed should, reject rule B, since it is false. Its falsehood, however, does not help demonstrate the necessary existence of that being who *alone* must exist if he is possible.

5

Finally, Professor Clarke opts for "expedience" in deciding whether or not to accept a theological theory.[24] He may have overlooked an aspect of expedience which is consistency with other theories we may also find fruitful. In addition to spelling out the purposes of a theoretical theology, anyone constructing such a theory must also show how to articulate it with other theories we may hold. Professor Ziff has suggested that any theory of a limitless God will conflict with any physical theory we are likely to hold.[25] I would appreciate Professor Clarke's comments on this further aspect of theory evaluation.

Notes

1. Page references in the following notes, unless otherwise noted, are to Professor Clarke's essay.

2. G. W. Leibniz, *Selections*, ed. Philip P. Wiener (New York: Scribner's, 1951), pp. 541–542, quoted by Clarke, pp. 44–45.

3. P. 45.

4. P. 45.

5. The conditions appear on page 45 and again on pages 48–52; rule C is discussed on p. 54.

6. I am treating, with Clarke, 'true' and 'false' as short for 'true (false) in theory T' and as equivalent to 'deductive consequence of T' and 'deductively inconsistent with T'. See, e.g., his discussion of rule A on pp. 48–51.

7. Henry S. Leonard and Nelson Goodman, "The Calculus of Individuals and Its Uses," *The Journal of Philosophy*, 5 (1940): 45–55, cited by Clarke, p. 52.

8. P. 53.

9. In *Philosophical Turnings* (Ithaca, N.Y.: Cornell University Press, 1966), pp. 93–102.

10. P. 48.

11. Pp. 52–57.

12. P. 51.

13. Pp. 48–52.

14. Immanuel Kant, *Critique of Pure Reason*, trans. Norman Kemp Smith (London: Macmillan, 1963), p. 503, cited in Clarke, p. 49. I am grateful to W. D. Falk for his illuminating discussion of Kant and his help with the German.

15. Immanuel Kant, *Kritik der Reinen Vernunft* (Leipzig: Felix Neiner Verlag, 1930), p. 570, lines 2–7, A595–6.

16. Kant translation, p. 502, cited in Clarke, p. 50.

17. P. 50.

18. P. 50.

19. P. 50.

20. P. 50.

21. P. 50.

22. P. 51.

23. P. 65. I am grateful to Robert Herrick for his discussions of the logic of this part.

24. Pp. 57–59.

25. *Philosophical Turnings*, pp. 101–102.

ON CRITERIA OF
ONTOLOGICAL COMMITMENT

Charles S. Chihara

When it was the fashion to debunk traditional ontological questions as being pseudoproblems based upon misconceptions of ordinary language, Quine took the radical position that traditional ontological questions are "on a par with questions of natural science." [1] To make sense of ontological questions, Quine divided the question "What things or sorts of things exist?" into two separate questions: (1) What, according to a given theory, exists? (In Quinian terms: What are the *ontological commitments* of a given theory?) and (2) Which theories have we good reason to accept as true? Concerning the latter question, Quine did not maintain that there are simple tests or criteria for determining truth. However, he did claim that we can give rational grounds for accepting theories—even those that carry ontological commitment to such metaphysical entities as universals. Indeed, he claimed that we can give, in these cases, the same sorts of grounds that are used to support scientific hypotheses. For, according to Quine, the considerations that guide a person in his choice of scientific theories are, where rational, "pragmatic";[2] and pragmatic considerations may prompt us to accept theories that require quantification over such universals as numbers and classes:

> Numbers and classes are favoured by the power and facility which they contribute to theoretical physics and other systematic discourse about nature. Propositions and attributes are disfavoured by some irregular behavior in connection with identity and substitution. Considerations for and against existence are more broadly systematic, in these philosophical examples, than in the case of rabbits or unicorns or prime numbers between 10 and 20; but I am persuaded that the difference is a matter of degree.[3]

Thus Quine attempted to put question (2) within the arena of rational assessment. However, I shall concern myself in this paper with various attempts to provide a rational, objective criterion for answering questions of the first sort. Before beginning my discussion of Quine's criterion, I should like to take up an important but preliminary question: Of what, besides theories, is Quine's criterion supposed to enable us to determine the ontological commitments? On this question, Quine is not very clear. "Discourses," "forms of discourse," "doctrines," "remarks," and "sentences" are some of the answers he gives. What Quine means by "form of discourse" is also not very clear. Since his earliest papers on this topic were concerned with the ontological commitments of languages,[4] one might suppose that a form of discourse is some sort of language or language form (i.e., partially interpreted language). Thus, a typical first order language that has been interpreted by specifying some of the predicates might be considered a "form of discourse." However, as I shall indicate later on, difficulties result from assuming that Quine intended his criterion to apply to "forms of discourse" in this sense. I shall avoid some of these problems by assuming in this paper that the criterion is to be applied to theories and sentences.

There are also some problems connected with Quine's use of the term "theory." [5] Quine says, in *Word and Object* and related writings, that a theory is a class of all those sentences "within some limited vocabulary appropriate to the desired subject matter" that a person believes to be true (or that some imaginary person might believe to be true); and he goes on to say that a theory need not be deductively closed.[6] However, elsewhere he writes: "A theory, it will be said, is a set of fully interpreted sentences. (More particularly, it is a deductively closed set.)" [7] Since the passages that follow this quotation strongly suggest that Quine accepts the above characterization of theories, it would appear that, at least some of the time, a theory for Quine must be deductively closed. For purposes of simplicity and convenience, I shall regard theories as deductively closed in this paper. (All of my main points would apply, with some small revisions, even if theories were not deductively closed.)

On many occasions, Quine has applied his criterion to single sentences. Since Quine sometimes suggests that his criterion was devised for determining the ontological commitments of *theories*, one might suppose that, for Quine, a single sentence is a kind of degenerate theory. Another reasonable hypothesis is that Quine's statements about the ontological commitments of some sentence is intended to be a statement about the commitments of some imagined theory asserting that sentence.

Quine has emphasized on several occasions that his criterion is meant only for those theories in quantificational form. Suppose then that we have some standard *uninterpreted* first order quantificational language. How are we supposed to get the sort of fully interpreted theory that Quine talks about? The following quotation provides us with the answer: "In specifying a theory we must indeed fully specify, in our own words, what sentences are to comprise the theory, and what things are to be taken as values of the variables, and what things are to be taken as satisfying the predicate letters." [8] Hence, to specify a theory in Quine's sense of the term, we need only select, from a first order language, a set of assertions (not containing individual constants) and supply an interpretation of the relevant portion of the language by specifying what is to be the universe of discourse and which English predicates or "interpretive expressions" (to use Quine's terminology) [9] are to be assigned to the predicate letters of the theory. [10] In the following, I shall refer to theories, interpreted as Quine requires, as "Quinian theories" or simply as "theories."

Now what is meant by "ontological commitment"? To put it another way: What is Quine's criterion supposed to be a criterion of? Quine presents us with a variety of *different* answers to this question. Let me list some of them. It is a criterion for determining what a theory (a) *presupposes* that there is; (b) *explicitly* presupposes that there is; (c) *implies* that there is; (d) *says* that there is. [11] Since, in general, what a theory presupposes that there is differs from what it implies that there is and from what it explicitly presupposes that there is; and these in turn differ from what the theory says that there is, my initial reaction to Quine's criterion was one of scepticism. [12] Quine may not have been entirely satisfied with his own groping attempts to explicate the point of his criterion, for in a more recent paper he says: "To show that a theory assumes a given object, or objects of a given class, we have to show that the theory would be false if that object did not exist, or if that class were empty; hence, that the theory requires that object, or members of that class, in order to be true. How are such requirements revealed?" [13] Later on in the paper, Quine answers his question: the objects that a theory "requires" are "those objects that have to be values of variables for the theory to be true".[14] Thus, Quine states his well-known criterion of ontological commitment.[15] Notice that in the above quotation, Quine talks about what a theory *requires*. It would now seem that what he is trying to develop is a criterion for determining what objects, or sorts of objects, a theory *requires* in order that it be true. Now why should we need a criterion for this purpose? Each Quinian theory is supplied with an interpretation that tells us what the universe of discourse of the theory is. Then, if the interpretation tells us that the variables range over, say natural numbers, can we not say that the theory requires natural numbers in order that its assertions be true, and hence is ontologically committed to natural numbers? A misunderstanding regarding Quine's use of the term "ontological commitment" needs to be cleared up:

> The trouble comes of . . . identifying the ontology of a theory with the class of all things to which the theory is ontically committed. . . . The ontology is the range of the variables. Each of the various reinterpretations of the range (while keeping the interpretations of predicates fixed) might be compatible with the theory. But the theory is ontically *committed* to an object only if that object is common to all those ranges. And the theory is ontically committed to "objects of such and such kind," say dogs, just in case each of those ranges contains some dog or other.[16]

It appears, from this quotation, that in determining the ontological commitments of a theory, we need not give any special weight to the particular universe of discourse specified by the interpretation—which explains why Quine applies his criterion to such sentences as '$(\exists x)$ (x is a dog)' without specifying any domain for the variable. From the point of view of a theory's ontological commitments, it makes no difference whether or not the theory comes with a specified universe of discourse.[17]

The above quotation was not meant to give us a criterion of ontological commitment; rather it was intended to explain the difference between the ontology and the ontological commitments of a theory. Still, the quotation warrants further examination. Suppose that we have a theory that asserts '$(\exists x)$ (x is a unicorn)', and suppose that the universe of discourse of this theory is specified to be the class of living animals. The ontology of this theory, it would seem, is the class of living animals. But does this ontology contain unicorns? Certainly, the class of living animals does not contain any unicorns. On the other hand, reasoning from the many examples Quine has given us, it is evident that such a theory is ontologically committed to unicorns. So are we to say that this theory is ontologically committed to a kind of entity none of which belong to the ontology of the theory? Another difficulty is suggested by the above quotation. It would seem that all the possible ranges that can be assigned to the variables of the theory, that keep the interpretation of the predicates fixed, and that are compatible with the theory, must contain unicorns; and this suggests that the original range assigned, viz, the class of living animals, must also contain unicorns. Take another example. Suppose a theory is interpreted to have as its domain the class of unicorns. The class of unicorns is the null set. So is the ontology of this theory the class of unicorns? Or does the theory have no ontology? Despite the many attempts Quine has made to clarify his ideas on ontology and ontological commitment, I for one would like to see further clarifications made.

Perhaps we should return to Quine's statement of his criterion for more illumination. Recall that the criterion is supposed to enable us to determine what objects a theory requires in order that it be true. The question arose: Why do we need a criterion for this purpose? Why not say that the objects the theory requires are just those objects that (according to the theory) would have to exist in order that it be true? I suppose it would be said in reply that there are two expressions that are vague in the above suggestion: (1) 'would have to' and (2) 'exist'. *We still need a criterion to tell us what would have to exist (according to the theory) in order that the theory be true.* Now what is Quine's proposed criterion? The sorts of objects that would have to exist in order that the theory be true are just those sorts of objects that would have to be within the range of the bound variables of the theory in order that its assertions be true. But what progress have we made? We still have the vague notion 'would have to' and instead of the term 'exist' we have the expression 'be within the range of the bound variables'. At first glance, it is hard to see why Quine would claim that he has given us a *criterion*. The difference between the *explicans* and the *explicandum* is so slight that one may wonder at the use of the term 'criterion' to mark the difference. Thus, one might say to Quine: If we need a *criterion* to determine what would have to exist in order that a theory be true, surely we also need a criterion to determine what would have to be values of the variables in order that the theory be true.

By way of contrast, let us examine a statement of a criterion of ontological commitment that more clearly deserves the title 'criterion'. Church states his own criterion as follows: "The assertion of $(\exists x)(M)$ carries ontological commitment to entities x such that M," where the letter 'x' may be replaced by any variable, the italicized letter '*x*' may be replaced by any name of the same variable, the letter 'M' may be replaced by any open sentence containing only the above variable, and the italicized letter '*M*' may be replaced by any name of this open sentence.[18] (Of course, the usual notational conventions apply so that, for example, '$(\exists x)$('*x* is a horse')' denotes '$(\exists x)$(x is a horse)'.)[19]

Here we are given a clear and definite test for ontological commitment. We can determine definitely that the assertion '$(\exists x)$ (*x* is a horse)' carries ontological commitment to entities *x* such that *x* is a horse. By this criterion, we also know that '$(\exists x)$ (*x* is a ghost)' is ontologically committed to ghosts and not to unicorns. In general we need only look at the existential assertions of a first order Quinian theory in order to determine its ontological commitments.

I should mention here that Chomsky and Scheffler state a criterion that is very similar to the above. They present the following criterion: "A theory T makes a _____-assumption if and only if it yields a statement of the form '$(\exists x)$ (*x* is (a) _____)'." [20] However, in this paper, I shall not concern myself with this version since it is so similar to Church's criterion.

To obtain some idea of how Quine applies his criterion, consider a second order theory in which it is valid to infer

$(\exists F)(\exists G)(\exists x)(Fx \& Gx)$

from

$(\exists x)$ (*x* is a dog & *x* is white).

According to Quine, the assertion of the latter sentence in a first order theory does not involve commitment to such abstract entities as dogkind or whiteness, whereas the second order theory does ontologically commit itself to these abstract entities by asserting the latter sentence.[21] The essential idea behind this application of the criterion is to be found in Quine's earliest articles on ontological commitment. For example it is asserted that: "What entities there are, from the point of view of a given language, depends on what positions are accessible to variables in that language." [22] Quine applies this early version of his criterion to draw a distinction between nominalistic and realistic languages: "Words of the abstract or general sort, say 'appendicitis' or 'horse', can turn up in nominalistic as well as realistic languages; but the difference is that in realistic languages such words are substituents for variables . . . whereas in nominalistic languages this is not the case." [23]

In these early articles, Quine concentrated primarily on the ontological commitments of *languages*, in contradistinction to theories, as can be seen from the above quotes. In expanding his criterion to cover theories, he had to go beyond mere accessibility to variables and take account of the *assertions* of theories. But he did not completely abandon his early views, as can be seen from the above example. Essentially, it was by applying his later criterion along the lines laid down by his earliest articles on the topic that Quine was led to charge the formal theory of *Principia Mathematica* with an ontological commitment to abstract entities. But who would have guessed from the formula "what would have to be values of the variables . . ." that we could apply the criterion in this way?

Now Quine has made two rather large claims for his criterion. The first is that ontological commitment belongs to "the theory of reference" rather than "the theory of meaning." [24] The precise nature of this claim is not clear since the distinction between theory of reference and theory of meaning is only roughly made by Quine in terms of some examples: the notions of synonymy, significance, analyticity and entailment, he tells us, belong to the theory of meaning, whereas truth, denotation, extension, and naming belong to the theory of reference. In this paper, Quine goes on to say that if a concept were to be defined using concepts from both areas, "we should probably reckon the hybrid concept to the theory of meaning—simply because the theory of meaning is in a worse state than the theory of reference. . . ." [25] One might conclude from this last statement that ontological commitment, as Quine "defines" it with his statement of his criterion, does not fall within the theory of reference, on the grounds that the phrase 'would have to', which appears in the statement, involves concepts taken from the theory of meaning. It should be noted that when Quine made the above claims, he did state a kind of criterion of ontological commitment that could be reasonably reckoned to the theory of reference: ". . . . to say that a given existential quantification presupposes objects of a given kind is to say simply that the open sentence which follows the quantifier is true of some objects of that kind and none not of that kind." [26] However, it is easy to see that this criterion yields some very counterintuitive results. For example, a theory might assert '$(\exists x)$ (x is a ghost)' and still not be committed to ghosts.[27] It is not surprising that Quine has dropped this version of the criterion.

Actually, the claim that ontological commitment belongs to the theory of reference has been thoroughly criticized by Cartwright.[28] Since Quine has never replied to the criticism and since he has not repeated his claim, one might infer that Quine has abandoned this early position. But to admit that ontological commitment belongs to that discredited area, the theory of meaning, is tantamount to admitting that ontological commitment is, itself, a muddled and unclear notion, in the same boat as the discredited notions of analyticity and meaning—something that Quine could hardly accept with an easy conscience.

The second large claim that Quine has made for his criterion is that ontological commitment "becomes objective and free of the old-time question-begging, once the theory is rendered in quantificational form." [29] To one contemplating Quine's vague statement of his criterion, it is by no means obvious that ontological commitment has become objective and free from question-begging.

Surprisingly, there is less doubt that Church's criterion satisfies the above two claims that Quine has made for his own criterion. Church's criterion does seem to fall within the theory of reference, since it makes no use of terms like 'necessity', 'meaning', and 'analyticity'. And the criterion is objective. I am not sure I would call it nonquestion-begging, but that may be because I am not sure I understand Quine's claim in this regard. Seeing how much better Church's criterion satisfies Quine's claims, it is reasonable to wonder why Quine, himself, did not adopt Church's version of the criterion. I suspect that the reason is: Church's criterion is, in certain respects, counterintuitive, being too stingy in handing out ontological commitments. For example, one cannot conclude that the assertion '$(\exists x)(x$ is a bachelor$)$' is committed to male human beings. And strictly interpreted, Church's criterion does not allow us to say that '$(\exists x)(x$ is a set$)$' carries ontological commitment to an entity x such that x is an abstract entity. I should think, to Quine, these consequences of adopting Church's criterion would be more than counterintuitive: they would make ontological commitment seem utterly trivial. Thus, we could claim that the usual Platonic set theories are not ontologically committed to abstract entities, on the grounds that the predicate 'abstract entity' does not occur in the vocabulary of the theory.

Unlike Church's criterion, Quine's allows us to go "outside" the target theory in determining ontological commitments. Quine tells us:

> there is certainly commitment to entities through discourse; for we are quite capable of saying in so many words that *there are* black swans, that *there is* a mountain more than 8800 meters high, and that *there are* prime numbers above a hundred. Saying these things, we also say by implication that there are physical objects and abstract entities; for all the black swans are physical objects and all the prime numbers above a hundred are abstract entities.[30]

By Quine's criterion, the standard mathematical theories are ontologically committed to abstract entities even though they do not explicitly say there are such things. Quine tells us in various places that the standard set theories are committed to universals. Why? Certainly, Quine did not think that by looking through a list of the theses of the theories, we would eventually find '$(\exists x)(x$ is a universal$)$'. However, Quine thinks we can assert

$(x)(\ (\exists y)(\exists z)(y \in x\ \&\ x \in z) \rightarrow x$ is a set$)$

and

$(x)(x$ is a set $\rightarrow x$ is a universal$)$.

Evidently, we are allowed to use these universal affirmative sentences in determining ontological commitments.

The problem we now face is this: Which, or what kinds of, statements are we allowed to use in determining ontological commitments? The sentences that Quine uses in "going outside the theory" are all universal affirmative sentences. Are we restricted to such sentences? But before examining this "syntactical" aspect of the question, I should like to explore the problem from the "semantical" point of view. Can we use any *true* universal affirmative sentence? Quine's vague statements of his criterion do not help us much to answer this question. Let us explore this possibility by tracing some of the consequences of allowing all true universal affirmative sentences to be used. As I have pointed out,[31] one unintuitive consequence of this interpretation is this: A theory affirming '$(\exists x)$ (x is a chair & x was manufactured in 1966 by Lane Furniture Co.)' would be ontologically committed to walnut chairs if all chairs manufactured by the company in 1966 were, as a matter of fact, made of walnut. Another unintuitive consequence is connected with the fact that '(x) (x is a ghost $\rightarrow$ x is a unicorn)' is a true sentence. A theory affirming '$(\exists x)$ (x is a ghost)' would thus be ontologically committed to unicorns. Other problems result from interpreting the criterion in the above manner. Quine holds that set theory is ontologically committed to universals; and I am sure he would deny that it is committed to unicorns. To obtain these results, we must hold that '(x) (x is a set $\rightarrow$ x is a universal)' is true, and that '(x) (x is a set $\rightarrow$ x is a unicorn)' is false. Since the latter is true if '-$(\exists x)$ (x is a set)' is true, we must hold that nominalism is false. In this case, we seem to be begging the question in favor of Platonism. I think it is clear that Quine would not accept these consequences: some other line must be drawn between the allowable and unallowable sentences.

Intuitively speaking, we wish to use only those universal affirmative sentences that are *necessarily true* or analytic: this is suggested by Quine's words "would have to be values of the variables" and also by the fact that the examples Quine gives us all seem to be sentences that would be classified by many philosophers as analytic or necessary truths. However, since Quine rejects the distinctions between analytic and synthetic statements and between necessary and contingent truths, this road does not appear to be open to him.

At this point, it is enlightening to compare Chateaubriand's criterion of ontological commitment with Quine's.[32] Chateaubriand suggests that we bypass the problem of distinguishing the class of necessary truths from the class of contingent truths by making use of the notion of theorems of a theory. For example, instead of talking about the necessary truths of arithmetic, we can talk about the theorems of arithmetic. By this maneuver, Chateaubriand has come up with an ersatz Quinian criterion of ontological commitment. He reasoned that since such terms as "implication" and "validity" had been defined for formal languages in terms of, or relative to, a meta-theory (which includes some set theory), he might be able to do something analogous for "ontological commitment." Why not define a criterion of ontological commitment relative to a meta-theory? At this point, I shall deviate somewhat from Chateaubriand's procedure and restrict my discussion of the criterion to first order Quinian theories the interpretations of which are given by English, supplemented by various notational devices. This restriction will enable me to formulate the criterion along the lines taken by Church and to avoid some of the complications in Chateaubriand's formulation.[33] Then we can state Chateaubriand's criterion by means of a schema in which the letters 'S' and 'T' are to be replaced by names of theories, the letter 'x' is to be replaced by any variable, the italicized letter 'x' is to be replaced by any name of the same variable, the letter 'F' is to be replaced by any open sentence containing only the above variable as a free variable, and the italicized letter 'F' is to be replaced by any name of this open sentence. We shall say that S carries ontological commitment to an entity x such that F (relative to meta-theory T) if and only if for some open sentence M, replacing the occurrences of the italicized letter 'M' in I and II below with occurrences of a name of M results in true sentences:

   I. $(\exists x)(M)$ is an assertion of S

   II. $(x)(M \rightarrow F)$ is an assertion of T.

Returning to the problem I raised earlier regarding Quine's criterion, Chateaubriand's suggestion comes to this: Those universal affirmative sentences we are allowed to use are simply those that are assertions of the relevant meta-theory. Thus, a standard set theory will carry ontological commitment to universals—relative to a meta-theory whose set of assertions contains '(x) ($(\exists y)$ $(\exists z)$ $(y \in x \,\&\, x \in z) \rightarrow x$ is a universal)'.

The above suggestion of Chateaubriand's was first sketched in my paper.[34] Shortly after the publication of this paper, Quine delivered the John Dewey Lectures at Columbia,[35] in which he presented his new doctrine of *ontological relativity*: roughly, the doctrine that we can meaningfully ask about the reference of terms in some language only relative to some "background language," and we can ask about the ontology of a theory only relative to some "background theory with its own primitively adopted and ultimately inscrutable ontology." [36] He argued that it makes no sense to say what the objects of a theory are "absolutely speaking"; we can only ask "how one theory of objects is interpretable or reinterpretable in another." [37] And he claimed that if, in specifying a Quinian theory, we say what the domain is and what the predicates are, we interpret the theory relative to our words and hence relative to our home language and the "over-all home theory" which lies behind this language.[38] Despite the fact that this doctrine suggests a similar thesis of the relativity of ontological commitment, Quine did not discuss his criterion. I should think it would be natural to try to develop some sort of Chateaubriand-type criterion of ontological commitment relative to this "over-all home theory" Quine talks about in his lectures. It is possible that Quine is moving in this direction. Recall that the universal affirmative sentences Quine used in determining ontological commitments were all sentences that would be classified as analytic by many philosophers. Now Quine rejects the analytic-synthetic distinction, but he does accept an "approximation": he says that a community-wide belief (or sentence accepted as true by the whole linguistic community) is his nearest approximation to an analytic sentence.[39] The idea of community-wide beliefs, although vague and sketchy, seems to provide us with a likely candidate for the class of assertions of the "over-all home theory" relative to which we can ask about the ontologies of theories we specify. But I only conjecture here since Quine has not specifically said at any time, so far as I know, that he is dissatisfied with his own statements of his criterion.

Let us return to the "syntactical" question we raised earlier: Are we allowed to use only universal affirmative sentences in determining ontological commitments by Quine's criterion? Or can we use other forms of sentences? This question can be clarified in terms of Chateaubriand's criterion. According to this criterion, we may use only assertions of T of the form '$(x)\ (M \to F)$' in determining the ontological commitments of S relative to T. But does it not seem somewhat arbitrary to restrict the criterion in this way? Suppose, for example, that a sentence of the form '$(\exists x)(M) \to (\exists x)(F)$' occurs among the assertions of T. If S asserts

$(\exists x)(M)$, then it would be natural to say that S is ontologically committed to an entity x such that F relative to T. If we follow our intuitions on this point, we get Chateaubriand's second criterion of ontological commitment relative to a meta-theory. In the following, 'Chateaubriand's criterion' will refer to this second version unless otherwise indicated. But what of Quine's criterion? It is difficult to tell whether we are allowed to use sentences of the form '$(\exists x)(M) \rightarrow (\exists x)(F)$' from Quine's statements of his criterion. I have argued that one could reasonably interpret Quine in either way: on one reasonable interpretation, a theory asserting

(A.) $(\exists x)(x$ is a winged-horse)

would be ontologically committed to wings, whereas on the other interpretation, the theory need not be.[40] Evidently, some philosophers have misunderstood my criticism, for objections have been raised that the lack of clarity I claimed to find in Quine's statements is due merely to the uncertainties that exist as to how we should paraphrase English predicates like 'is a winged-horse'. But I am not asking if (A) can be paraphrased into

(B.) $(\exists x)(x$ is a horse & $(\exists y)(y$ is a wing & x has $y))$.

My question is about how to apply Quine's criterion, and it will not be answered by the statement that (A) can be paraphrased into (B). Fortunately, since the publication of my earlier paper, Quine has clarified his position. The problem is: How are we to understand the words 'such and such objects have to be values of the variables in order for the theory to be true'? Quine tells us that, for theories that include a complementary predicate for each predicate, the above words say the same thing as 'the predicates of the theory have to be true of such and such objects in order for the theory to be true'.[41]

To see how Quine's recent statement decides my 'winged-horse' question, notice that 'x is a winged-horse' cannot be true of wings. If we allow that (A) can be true, it follows that 'x is a winged-horse' need not be true of wings in order that (A) be true. It follows that (A) is not ontologically committed to wings. From this, we see that Quine has chosen a criterion that is closer to Chateaubriand's first criterion than to the second. It leads to some rather counterintuitive results.

To see this more clearly, let us suppose that we construct a theory which asserts

(C.) $(\exists x)(x$ is a full set of golf clubs $)$.

And suppose that we explicate (in the meta-theory) the predicate 'is a full set of golf clubs' by asserting that a full set of golf clubs must contain nine irons and four woods. We can see that (C) is true only if there are golf clubs (indeed, irons and woods). But since the predicate 'is a full set of golf clubs' cannot be true of golf clubs, by Quine's criterion, (C) cannot be ontologically committed to them. What all this suggests is that Quine's criterion give us, at best, sufficient conditions of ontological commitment rather than necessary and sufficient conditions as he claims.

One of my colleagues has recently raised an objection to Quine's criterion that bears on this last point. Searle claims to show that "there is no substance to" Quine's criterion.[42] And he purports to construct a "*reductio ad absurdum* of the criterion." [43] The argument proceeds as follows: Let '*K*' be an abbreviation for a conjunction of statements which state all existing scientific knowledge. (We can take *K* to be the conjunction of all statements in some encyclopedia.) We define the predicate '*P*' as follows:

Px if and only if $x = $ this pen & K.

Proof: 1. This pen $=$ this pen   (axiom)
  2. K (axiom)
  3. $\therefore$ This pen $=$ this pen & K
  4. $\therefore$ P (this pen)
  5. $\therefore$ $(\exists x)Px$

Searle then writes: "Thus, in the spirit of Q's ontological reduction we demonstrate that, in terms of Q's criterion of ontological commitment, the only commitment needed to assert the whole of established scientific truth is a commitment to the existence of this pen. But this is a *reductio ad absurdum* of the criterion." [44] What are we to make of this argument? I must confess I still find it difficult to see the point of the above "proof" of '$(\exists x)Px$' from the axioms. At first, I thought Searle was arguing that one can deduce 5. from 1. and 2., that 5. is only ontologically committed to this pen, and that therefore 2. is only ontologically committed to this pen. But this reasoning is too absurd to be taken seriously. I have since learned from Searle that the proof was meant to show how '$(\exists x)Px$' is "based upon" the conjunction K. Although I am not sure I understand Searle on this point, it is clear to me now that the deduction is not essential to his argument. The main point of his *reductio* comes to this: Consider a theory, U, the set of axioms of which contains only '$(\exists x)Px$'. By Quine's criterion, U is ontologically committed to this pen, but not to cats, dogs, people, etc., the existence of which is clearly asserted, assumed, presupposed, or implied by the theory. Thus, we get a *reductio*.

Now there are many points that should be discussed in a full treatment of Searle's argument. But I wish to make only one point here: The force of Searle's argument is greatly reduced if Quine admits (as I believe he should) that his criterion provides only sufficient conditions of ontological commitment and not necessary and sufficient conditions as it is supposed (and claimed).

It is not so clear that Searle's argument damages Chateaubriand's second criterion. If we get counterintuitive results from this criterion, it may be due to our choice of theories rather than to the criterion itself. This can be seen by making use of some ideas in Quine's John Dewey Lectures. To construct a Quinian theory, we must specify the predicates of the theory, i.e., we must either say (in a meta-language) what the predicates are or assign predicates (interpretive expressions) from the meta-language to the predicate letters of the formal language of the theory. So a Quinian theory presupposes, as it were, what Quine calls a "background language" and a "background theory." It would be natural then to seek the ontological commitments of a Quinian theory relative to its background theory. For example, if we construct a theory V, that asserts

$(\exists x)(x$ is a bottle of acid$)$

the predicates 'is an acid', 'is acidic', 'is a proton donor', and 'yields hydronium ions in water solution' need not even occur in the vocabulary of the theory; yet they are predicates of the background language (in this case: English) and the background theory. And it is reasonable to suppose that chemistry would be part of this background theory. So that we might be able to say something definite about the ontological commitments of V relative to any reasonable formulation of the background theory (making use of Chateaubriand's criterion). Or take the case of a theory that asserts '$(\exists x)(x$ is an infinite set of prime numbers$)$', but that has a vocabulary not containing the predicate 'is an odd number'. The background theory can be expected to include the usual theorems and laws of number theory. So we could argue, using Chateaubriand's criterion, that this theory is committed to odd numbers relative to any reasonable formulation of the background theory. Turning to Searle's theory, we can say that any reasonable formulation of its background theory will assert such things as

$(\exists x)\, Px \to (\exists x)\, (x \text{ is a cat})$

so that we can expect this strange theory to be ontologically committed to cats, dogs, people, etc., after all—but relative to a reasonable formulation of its background theory. Of course, the notion of a background theory is, at this time, rather vague. But I anticipate further clarifications and developments of this idea from the pen of Quine.

In this paper, I have examined four criteria of ontological commitment. Of the four, I believe Chateaubriand's second criterion is the most adequate. This is not to say, however, that the criterion is entirely adequate. One difficulty with the criterion (and with other Church-type criteria) is that one ends up with some strange statements of ontological commitment. For example, it is easy to see that the criterion could tell us that:

(D) relative to W', W carries ontological commitment to an entity x such that $x = x$ and $(\exists y)\,(y$ is a golf club).

But what does (D) mean? It is not clear. One might understand it to mean that W is ontologically committed to something identical to itself and that there are golf clubs. Or one might read (D) as saying that W is ontologically committed to golf clubs. If we adopt the second reading, we shall run into another difficulty suggested to me by George Myro. Suppose that W asserts

$(\exists x)\,(x$ is a full set of golf clubs)

and that W' asserts

(E) $(\exists x)(x$ is a full set of golf clubs$) \to (\exists x)(x$ is a golf club)

but not

$(x)\,(x$ is a full set of golf clubs $\to x$ is a golf club).

Then we are inclined to think that, relative to W', W is ontologically committed to golf clubs according to the second criterion, but not so committed according to the first. However, (E) is equivalent to

$(x)\,(x$ is a full set of golf clubs $\to x = x$ & $(\exists y)\,(y$ is a golf club)). So if we do adopt a policy of giving sentences like (D) the second type of reading, we shall have to say that the first and second Chateaubriand criteria come to essentially the same thing. We can eliminate some of these problems with strange commitments by tightening up the criteria so that the open sentence *F* must be quantifier-free. But this way of dealing with the problem produces other counterintuitive results.

Quine once wrote:

> But it is to the familiar quantificational form of discourse that our criterion of ontological commitment primarily and fundamentally applies. To insist on the correctness of the criterion in this application is, indeed, merely to say that no distinction is being drawn between the "there are" of "there are universals," "there are unicorns," "there are hippopotami," and the "there are" of "($\exists x$)," "there are entities *x* such that." To contest the criterion, as applied to the familiar quantificational form of discourse, is simply to say either that the familiar quantificational notation is being re-used in some new sense (in which case we need not concern ourselves) or else that the familiar "there are" of "there are universals" et al. is being re-used in some new sense (in which case again we need not concern ourselves).[45]

Quine must have been confused when he made this claim. For, as we have seen, stating an adequate criterion of ontological commitment is not as simple as all that. In this paper, I have argued against the adequacy of Quine's criterion, and none of my arguments involve questioning the thesis that the existential quantifier has the sense of the English phrase 'there are'.

Notes

1. *From a Logical Point of View*, 2nd ed. (New York: Harper and Row, 1961), p. 45.

2. Ibid., p. 46.

3. Donald Davidson and Jaako Hintikka, eds., *Words and Objections: Essays on the Work of W. V. Quine*, (Dordrecht, Holland: D. Reidel, 1969), pp. 97–98.

4. "Designation and Existence," *Journal of Philosophy* 36 (1939):701–709, and "A Logistical Approach to the Ontological Problem," printed for distribution in 1939 at the fifth International Congress for the Unity of Science. Reprinted in *The Ways of Paradox and Other Essays* (New York: Random House, 1966).

5. In my paper "Our Ontological Commitment to Universals," *Nous* 2 (1968): 25–46, I have noted some of the difficulties of interpretation, connected with Quine's criterion, that arose because Quine was so inexpli-

86 / CHARLES S. CHIHARA

cit about his use of the term "theory." Fortunately, since the publication of that paper, Quine has clarified his use of this term in at least two places.

6. Davidson and Hintikka, p. 309.

7. *Ontological Relativity and Other Essays* (New York: Columbia University Press, 1969), p. 51.

8. Ibid.

9. *From a Logical Point of View*.

10. Predicates, in Quine's sense of this term, are considered by him to be interpretive expressions (ibid., p. 136). In this paper, the logical notation and terminology will be that of Benson Mates in *Elementary Logic* (New York: Oxford University Press, 1965) unless otherwise indicated.

11. See Chihara, "Our Ontological Commitment to Universals," pp. 28–29.

12. Ibid., pp. 29–30.

13. Davidson and Hintikka, *Words and Objections*, p. 93.

14. Ibid., p. 96.

15. The expression "ontological commitment" is to be found in Quine's early papers on this topic. In *Word and Object* Quine began to use the term "ontic commitment." In this paper, I shall stick to the former term.

16. Davidson and Hintikka, *Words and Objections*, p. 315.

17. Cf. my conjecture in "Our Ontological Commitment to Universals," p. 65, as to what Quine means by "theory." That article was written before the above clarifying remarks of Quine's appeared.

18. Alonzo Church, "Ontological Commitment," *Journal of Philosophy* 55 (1958): 1014.

19. Mates, *Elementary Logic*, chap. 2.

20. Noam Chomsky and Israel Scheffler, "What Is Said to Be," *Proceedings of the Aristotelian Society* 59 (1958–1959): 79.

21. *From a Logical Point of View*, pp. 113, 120–122.

22. *The Ways of Paradox and Other Essays*, (New York: Random House, 1966), p. 68.

23. Herbert Feigl and Wilfrid Sellars, eds., *Readings in Philosophical Analysis* (New York: Appleton-Century-Crofts, 1949), p. 50.

24. *From a Logical Point of View*, pp. 130–131.

25. Ibid., p. 130.

26. Ibid., p. 131.

27. Essentially, this point was made by Richard L. Cartwright in "Ontology and the Theory of Meaning," *Philosophy of Science* 21 (1954): 323.

28. Ibid., pp. 316–325.

29. "The Philosophical Bearing of Modern Logic," in *Philosophy in the Mid-Century: A Survey*, ed. Raymond Klibansky (Florence: La Nuova Italia, 1958), p. 3.

30. *The Ways of Paradox and Other Essays*, p. 128.

31. "Our Ontological Commitment to Universals," pp. 33–34.

32. Oswaldo Chateaubriand's criterion is set forth in detail in his Ph.D. dissertation, "*Ontic Commitment, Ontological Reduction and Ontology*," University of California, Berkeley, 1971.

33. Obviously, about those theories to which this version of the criterion does not apply, the criterion says nothing. In particular, it does *not* say that higher order theories are not ontologically committed to universals, sets, concepts, etc. (relative to some other theory).

34. "Our Ontological Commitment to Universals."

35. Reprinted in *Ontological Relativity and Other Essays.*

36. Ibid., p. 51.

37. Ibid., p. 201.

38. Davidson and Hintikka, *Words and Objections*, p. 202.

39. Ibid., p. 310.

40. "Our Ontological Commitment to Universals."

41. *Ontological Relativity and Other Essays*, p. 95.

42. John Searle, *Speech Acts: An Essay in the Philosophy of Language* (Cambridge: Cambridge University Press, 1969), p. 107.

43. Ibid., p. 110.

44. Ibid.

45. *From a Logical Point of View*, p. 105.

RESPONSE

Robert G. Burton

In his paper Professor Chihara examines four different criteria of ontological commitment. He begins with W. V. Quine's criterion and proceeds to argue that in several ways an alternative criterion proposed by Alonzo Church is less problematical. He then considers two additional criteria suggested by Oswaldo Chateaubriand, arguing that the first is an improvement over Church's criterion, and that the second is the most adequate of the four. Let me preface my remarks by saying that I find Professor Chihara's discussion insightful, and that, within the limits of the territory that he marks out for himself, there is relatively little with which I would wish to take strong issue. I might mention just two such items at this point before moving to the issue that will occupy the major part of my brief remarks. For one thing, in both his present paper and in an earlier one entitled "Our Ontological Commitment to Universals," [1] Chihara has labeled Quine a Platonist; this is surely contentious. In "Logic and the Reification of Universals" [2] Quine very reluctantly embraces conceptualism developing what amounts to a special theory of types to provide for the construction of classes only insofar as they admit of ordered generation. Surely the conceptualist's universe of classes is less bloated than the Platonist's. And furthermore, the conceptualist is under no illusions about *discovering* independently subsistent classes.

Another point that calls for direct comment is Professor Chihara's suggestion that Church's criterion is more successful than Quine's in satisfying the claims Quine makes for his criterion of falling within the theory of reference and of being objective. Chihara suggests that Quine's reason for not adopting Church's criterion may be the fact that Church's criterion is "too stingy in handing out ontological commitments." Now I should have thought that just the opposite was the case, i.e., that Church's criterion in effect commits one to McX's highly problematical and bloated universe of meanings.

But the point that I am most interested in raising here is one that will have the effect of challenging all four of the criteria considered by Chihara.

At the beginning of his paper, Chihara recalls that Quine distinguishes the question "What, according to a given theory, exists?" from the question "Which theories have we good reason to accept as true?" Quine holds that the only good or rational reasons that may guide a person in his choice of theories are *pragmatic* reasons.

> Physical objects are conceptually imported into the situation as convenient intermediaries—not by definition in terms of experience, but simply as irreducible posits comparable, epistemologically, to the gods of Homer. . . . Both sorts of entities enter our conception only as cultural posits. The myth of physical objects is epistemologically superior to most in that it has proved more efficacious than other myths as a device for working a manageable structure into the flux of experience.[3]

But the first of Quine's two questions purportedly asks, in a neutral tone of voice, "What are the ontological commitments of a given theory?" And Quine's criterion is offered as a means of answering that question. An axiologist might say that Quine's criterion is allegedly descriptive and not prescriptive. But, if it should turn out that Quine's criterion is not neutral after all, it would follow that the criterion would be unable to do its purely descriptive job. I would contend that not one of the four criteria examined by Chihara is neutral in the required sense, and that therefore not one of them can do the job for which it was created. This is neither the time nor the place to argue such a contention in any detail. Fortunately for us, the general point, at least as it applies to Quine's criterion, has already been admirably argued by a fellow symposiast, Professor Severens, and another symposiast, Professor Romane Clarke has noted though not argued the point. My point is essentially that the other three criteria examined by Professor Chihara are sufficiently similar to Quine's criterion to be vulnerable to the same objections. For example, Church's criterion is like Quine's in that it presupposes that whatever a theory says there is can be named, thus begging the question against Frege's theory committed to unnameable concepts and Everett Hall's theory committed to unnameable facts. It is interesting to note that Quine himself is not totally blind to his criterion's nonneutral character insofar as he acknowledges its "*polemical* use." [4]

But what are we to make of the charge of question begging? One plausible answer to this question may be suggested if we turn to Quine's new doctrine of *ontological relativity*. This new doctrine, first articulated in the John Dewey Lectures at Columbia in 1968, grows out of Quine's discovery that the inscrutability of meaning has an analogue, the inscrutability of reference. According to this doctrine, it is meaningless to ask about the reference of terms in a given theory absolutely; we can meaningfully ask this question only relative to some background theory. Compare this to relativity theory in physics. In the relational doctrine of space it is senseless to ask for absolute position or absolute velocity; it makes sense only to ask for position or velocity relative to some arbitrarily selected frame of reference. The regress of spatial coordinate systems is terminated in practice by something like pointing. In Quine's relational doctrine of what the objects of theories are it is impossible to say what the objects of a theory are absolutely; it makes sense only to say how to interpret or reinterpret one theory in another. In practice the regress of background theories usually ends when we reach our "over-all home theory" whose language is our "mother tongue" and whose words we simply take at face value. But since any background theory has its own primitively adopted and ultimately inscrutable ontology, the objects of any such theory including our over-all home theory can be questioned at will.[5]

Now in the light of this new doctrine one might expect Quine to replace his "absolute" criterion of ontological commitment with a "relativistic" one, and I share Professor Chihara's surprise in the fact that Quine makes no mention of his celebrated criterion in this paper. As a passing observation, I suspect that the seeds of Quine's recent discovery are to be found in his earlier works dating back more than twenty years. For example, in "Logic and the Reification of Universals" [6] Quine in his discussion of the ontological presuppositions of ordinary language seems clearly to anticipate his current views concerning background theories. In that early paper he joins the philosophical devotees of ordinary language "in doubting the final adequacy of any criterion of the ontological presuppositions of ordinary language. . . ." [7] But the point of central interest for our present concerns is this: if ontological commitment is necessarily commitment relative to some arbitrarily selected background theory or other, then there is no such thing as the ontological commitment of a given theory *per se*, and so there can be no criterion of it. But this amounts to saying that something like begging the question from the perspective of some background theory or other is unavoidable. And so since candidates for background theory do not come to us labeled "take me" or "the buck *necessarily* stops here," if there are grounds for accepting a given theory on a given occasion, they are presumably, "where rational, pragmatic." [8]

Notes

1. Charles S. Chihara, "Our Ontological Commitment to Universals," *Nous* 2 (1968): 25–46.

2. Willard Van Orman Quine, *From a Logical Point of View*, 2nd ed. (New York: Harper and Row, 1961), pp. 102–129.

3. Ibid., p. 44.

4. Ibid., p. 105.

5. Willard Van Orman Quine, "Ontological Relativity," *Journal of Philosophy* 65 (1968): 185–212.

6. Quine, *From a Logical Point of View*, pp. 102–129.

7. Ibid., p. 106.

8. Ibid., p. 46.

ONTIC CONTENT AND COMMITMENT

James Willard Oliver

Quine's criterion of ontic commitment is eminently reasonable. At least initially, it seems intuitively obvious and inescapable; applications are useful and important. Close reading of the texts, however, leaves ·one with several questions that call for an explication of the criterion, and it is the purpose of this paper to discuss some of these questions.

It should be noted at once that the criterion is to be distinguished from others of Quine's views related to ontology and language. The criterion is one thing; advocacy of paraphrasing as a method for eliminating commitment to unwanted entities is another; specific proposals for paraphrasing are a third; the advocacy of minimal ontologies is a fourth, and a pluralistic view of acceptable ontologies is still another. But the criterion may be discussed apart from these other issues.

The criterion is, of course, applicable only to interpreted theories in explicitly quantificational form, and the logic of the theories includes identity theory. Furthermore, Quine's distinctions (1) between the ontology of a theory and the ontic commitments of a theory, and (2) between the question of what there *is* and the question of what a theory *says* there is—the ontic commitment of the theory—should be observed. The ontology of a theory[1] is simply the range of values of the variables of the theory, whereas the ontic commitment of the theory is often only a part of this range. The ontology or range of values is a matter of the conceptual scheme or language system in which the theory is stated,[2] but ontic commitment is a matter of the separate theories expressed in a conceptual scheme. Of two theories in the same conceptual scheme—that is, having the same ontology—one may be committed to the Parthenon and not to the Seagram Building, while the commitments of the other are just the reverse.

Questions as to what a theory *says* there is and what there *is* are largely independent. The ontic commitments of a theory are (at least roughly) a matter of logic, and the criterion is equally applicable to every one of a group of incompatible theories. Considerations of pragmatics, on the other hand, enter into decisions concerning what there is; within a group of incompatibile theories, epistemological considerations may be brought to bear in the selection of the one which is the acceptable view of what there actually is. To be sure, the ontic commitments of a theory may be used as a reason for assessing it as an unsatisfactory account of reality, but these commitments would rarely be the sole consideration.

To provide a basis for discussion, a review of Quine's wording of the criterion will be helpful. Of the many formulations, of varying exactness, a selection has been made. As early as 1939, in "A Logistical Approach to the Ontological Problem," the criterion is stated "elliptically":

> We may be said to countenance such and such an entity if and only if we regard the range of our variables as including such an entity.[3]

"Notes on Existence and Necessity," from 1943, contains the following remarks:

> The ontology which one accepts, or which a given context presupposes, is not revealed by an examination of mere vocabulary; for we know that substantives can be used indesignatively without depriving them of meaning. . . . It is not the mere use of a substantive, but its designative use, that commits us to the acceptance of an object designated by the substantive.[4]

Perhaps the best known formulations are from the 1948 paper, "On What There Is":

> The variables of quantification, 'something', 'nothing', 'everything', range over our whole ontology, whatever it may be; and we are convicted of a particular ontological presupposition if, and only if, the alleged presuppositum has to be reckoned among the entities over which our variables range in order to render one of our affimations true.[5]

We now have a more explicit standard whereby to decide what ontology a given theory or form of discourse is committed to:

a theory is committed to those and only those entities to which the bound variables of the theory must be capable of referring in order that the affirmations made in the theory be true.[6]

In 1950, *Methods of Logic* provided this wording:

The objects whose existence is implied in our discourse are finally just the objects which must, for the truth of our assertions, be acknowledged as "values of variables"—i.e., be reckoned into the totality of objects over which our variables of quantification range.[7]

The paper "Ontology and Ideology" of 1951 provides two statements:

The ontology to which an (interpreted) theory is committed comprises all and only the objects over which the bound variables of the theory have to be construed as ranging in order that the statements affirmed in the theory be true.[8]

The theory presupposes all and any of those entities whose nonoccurrence within the ranges of the variables of quantification would render parts of the theory false.[9]

In the 1953 version of "Logic and the Reification of Universals" the criterion was formulated as follows:

In general, an entity is assumed by a theory if and only if it must be counted among the values of the variables in order that the statements affirmed in the theory be true.[10]

In the second edition of *From a Logical Point of View*, 1961, this wording was changed to:

In general, entities of a given sort are assumed by a theory if and only if some of them must be counted among the values of the variables in order that the statements affirmed in the theory be true.[11]

"Notes on the Theory of Reference," also first published in 1953, considers a special case:

To say that a given existential quantification presupposes objects of a given kind is to say simply that the open sentence which follows the quantifier is true of some objects of that kind and none not of that kind.[12]

The latest wording appears in the 1968 paper, "Existence and Quantification":

> To show that a theory assumes a given object, or objects of a given class, we have to show that the theory would be false if that object did not exist, or if that class were empty; hence that the theory requires that object, or members of that class in order to be true.[13]

The quotations show an initial interest in the conditions under which a theory carries ontological commitment to a specific entity; later, conditions for commitment to entities of a given sort are considered, and finally the criterion becomes a double one, providing for both cases.

Though the wording varies, apparently any quantificational paraphrase of the criterion would be a universally quantified biconditional. Fitch[14] has remarked that it is strange to find in Quine's work what is apparently quantification over both classes and modalities; his comments need to be taken into account in any attempt at explication, but for the moment we call attention to the logical structure of the criterion only to display the part we wish to discuss next. What would appear in the first part of the biconditional of paraphrases of the formulations quoted above is such wording as 'is committed to', 'commits us to the acceptance of', 'presupposes', and 'assumes'. Now our first question is: *Is this fragment of the criterion, and thus the whole criterion, an assertion in pragmatics, or is the criterion to be regarded as belonging to semantics?* Quine uses such wording as 'we commit ourselves to an ontology containing numbers',[15] and 'we are convicted of a particular ontological presupposition'. Even if it is always a theory that does the committing, the verb itself suggests that a theory commits *a person* to something, and that the criterion is in pragmatics. At least one critic—Alston[16]—hoping to provide an improved statement, provides a formulation that is clearly in pragmatics. Furthermore, the term 'theory,' persistently used, with its suggestion of being a statement or a set of statements *asserted* or *believed* by someone, might contribute to the view that the concept of ontological commitment belongs to pragmatics.

But the evidence is in favor of construing it as not within pragmatics. In "On What There Is" Quine characterizes the aphoristic version of the criterion, 'To be is to be the value of a variable', as a "semantical formula." [17] Elsewhere he writes that the "criterion of ontological commitment applies in the first instance to discourse and not to men." [18] And in "Notes on the Theory of Reference" he remarks that "the notion of ontological commitment belongs to the theory of reference." [19] Also, more recent formulations use the words 'presuppose' and 'assume'; 'commit' appears in none of the more exact formulations of the criterion since 1951. And so far as the term 'theory' is concerned, it may be noted that any suggestion of a pragmatic character for this term is irrelevant in the context of Quine's ontological discussions. In his "Replies" in *Words and Objections*, Quine distinguishes a technical, nonpragmatic sense from a nontechnical, possibly pragmatic, sense used in his discussions of translation and language learning[20] but it is the former that is pertinent to the present paper. This is evident from an additional remark in "Ontological Relativity," [21] where a 'theory' is simply a deductively closed set of interpreted sentences. Furthermore, when we are concerned with what objects are assumed by a statement or set of statements, it is irrelevant whether anyone affirms or believes them. The criterion is equally applicable to 'Pegasus exists' and to 'Pegasus doesn't exist'. Quine's discussions do include many remarks in pragmatics related to the criterion, but these raise other issues (see question seven below); the criterion itself is concerned only with what might be called 'ontic content';[22] and calling it a 'criterion of ontic content' might help to avoid some confusion.

Denying the term 'theory' any pragmatic connotation leaves another small puzzle about Quine's use of the word in the formulations quoted. The second question is: *Is a theory just any statement or set of statements in explicitly quantificational form, or does it include all the implications of the statements that comprise it?* Quine's answer, from "Ontological Relativity," is: "A theory . . . is a set of fully interpreted sentences. (More particularly, it is a deductively closed set; it includes all its own logical consequences, insofar as they are couched in the same notation)." [23] But it is more convenient to allow the criterion of ontic content to apply to statements and sets of statements, not

necessarily including the logical consequences of these statements.[24] Our interest may frequently be in single statements. We
may wish to know what objects are assumed by the statement
'Everything is a physical object', or by 'The golden mountain
exists'; in applying the criterion there seems to be no need to
consider only deductively closed sets of statements, and if we
allow application to sets of statements as well as to single statements, the former may, whenever we wish, be sets that include
all their logical consequences. It is true that the ontic content of
a statement or a set of statements will, if the explication provided
later in this paper is satisfactory, be the same as those of the
corresponding theories, but it seems easier in the phrasing of
many applications to consider what entities a statement assumes,
rather than to have to speak of the theories of which the statement is the initial member. Quine's practice in a number of
specific cases conforms with the modification proposed.

Our third question has to do with the word 'assumes', which
we take to be the principal expression in the left half of the biconditional of the criterion: *What is the structure of the fragments of the criterion in which 'assumes' occurs?* As a technical
term, it seems to be a two-place predicate, and apparently its extension is a relation comprising pairs of statements (and sets of
statements) and objects, such as '$(\exists x) (x = \text{Fido})$' paired with
Fido, and the axioms of membership of Quine's system ML paired
with the natural number 2.

We immediately encounter two problems, the first of which has
to do with the rather awkward use of substantives in the plural
following 'assumes' in the fashion: 'a theory assumes objects of
a given sort'. Both Bar-Hillel and Fitch have been puzzled by
this wording. Bar-Hillel writes, "Is there any independent good
reason for taking the phrase 'there is an x such that' as seriously
as Quine does, and to infer from such a usage that whoever uses
this phrase commits himself to acknowledge the 'existence' of all
those entities of which the sentential schema following this phrase
is true?" [25] And Fitch remarks, "Does [the criterion] mean that *all*
entities of a given sort are assumed by a theory if and only if *some*
of them must be counted among the values of the variables . . . ?
This seems odd." [26] But the interpretation which Bar-Hillel and
Fitch find puzzling was, rather clearly, not Quine's intent. An
existential quantification surely will "assume" only some, not
necessarily all, objects of which the open sentence following the

quantifier is true. *If* (and only if) 'assumes' is a two-place predicate, can it occur in such metalinguistic statements as '$(\exists x)$ (Theorem 10 assumes $x \cdot x$ is a real number)', and can the criterion of ontic content for kinds of objects be phrased in the manner suggested to avoid plurals in the second place.

A more serious difficulty in construing 'assumes' as a two-place predicate with a relation as its extension arises in connection with examples such as: '$(\exists x)(x = \text{Pegasus})$' assumes Pegasus. What is wanted is that this be true. If, however, 'assumes' is a two-place predicate, the pair consisting of the statement and the alleged animal is in its extension. But since Pegasus doesn't exist, the pair is not in that extension. The conclusion is that 'assumes' is not a two-place predicate,[27] and the version of the criterion suitable for application to cases where objects of a given kind are concerned, just proposed, is unsatisfactory, since it uses 'assumes' as a two-place predicate.

No construction '$s \ldots a$' which *appears* to relate statements and sets of statements to entities and also has a true instance in which 'a' is replaced by a nondesignating singular term will actually succeed in making the relation. No such construction will have a relation as its extension, nor can it be construed as a combination of a two-place predicate (however complicated) with two singular terms.

Obviously, since such a construction with 'assumes' in the blank is not a "mode of containment"[28] at all, it is not a referentially opaque construction. But it is similar to the latter in that referentially opaque modes of containment are also not to be construed as predicates with one of their places corresponding to a position that is not purely referential.

It is interesting that it is not clear whether or not substitutivity of identity fails for the position 'a'. Intuitively perhaps one *wishes* this principle to hold, but the notion of assuming is sufficiently vague that there seem to be no clear-cut examples in which the principle either holds or fails. Thus applying the criterion for a purely referential position[29] does not tell us whether the position 'a' is purely referential. Even the considerations in the three preceding paragraphs seem only to show that sentences saying that certain statements assume specific entities do not have the structure that would justify application of the substitutivity principle—not that the principle if applied would fail.

An alternative interpretation of 'assumes' construes it as elliptical for 'assumes that there exists' or 'assumes that there exists a'.[30] The last example is construed as short for:

'$(\exists x)\ (x = $ Pegasus)' assumes that $(\exists x)\ (x = $ Pegasus)

and:

'$(\exists x)\ (x$ is-a-dog)' assumes dogs

is construed as:

'$(\exists x)\ (x$ is-a-dog)' assumes that $(\exists x)\ (x$ is-a-dog).

Generally, one version of the criterion will employ expressions of the following pattern:

1. s assumes that $(\exists x)(x = a)$.

and the objects-of-a-given-sort version will employ:

2. s assumes that $(\exists x)(Fx)$.

Here 's', 'a' and 'F' are schematic letters; 's' is replaceable by the names of statements, 'a' is replaceable by singular terms of the object language, and 'F' is replaceable by one place predicates of the object language.[31] (The wording 2 obviously eliminates the puzzle of Bar-Hillel and Fitch, without requiring quantification into what is, possibly, a referentially opaque construction.)

So much for the first part of the criterion. In connection with the other part, it should be noted that Quine's various wordings employ a subjunctive conditional and an assortment of apparently modal expressions: 'the theory would be false if the object did not exist,' [32] 'the alleged presuppositum has to be reckoned', [33] 'those entities to which the bound variables of the theory must be capable of referring' [34] 'the objects which must, for the truth of our assertions, be acknowledged.' [35] So our fourth question is: *Is there a satisfactory explication of the right half of the biconditional which employs no modalities or subjunctives?*

In "Existence and Quantification" Quine's discussion contains the essentials of such an explication for the version of the criterion applicable to specific objects, and it is a simple matter to provide an explication for the version for sorts or kinds of objects. For the former, the discussion proceeds as follows:

3. A theory assumes [that there exists] a if and only if it contains an expression which is (grammatically) a name of a and it uses this expression to name a.

But, since a theory *uses* an expression *to name* an object if and only if it "affirms" the existentially quantified identity built on that expression (i.e., '$(\exists x)(x = \ldots)$' with that expression inserted in the blank), 3 becomes, subject to some notational correction:

4. A theory assumes [that there exists] *a* if and only if it contains an expression which is (grammatically) a name of *a* and it affirms '$(\exists x)(x = a)$'.

Since, as noted earlier, a theory is for Quine a deductively closed set of statements, presumably what is meant here by 'affirms' is that '$(\exists x)(x = a)$' is a member of the set which is the theory. Also, since to say that a theory contains a name of *a* is simply to say that this name occurs in some statement in the theory, the first clause in the last part of 4 is redundant. 4 becomes, subject to notational correction:

5. A theory assumes [that there exists] *a* if and only if it has '$(\exists x)(x = a)$' as a member.

If the criterion is modified to permit application to statements and sets of statements rather than to theories only, the wording needs to be adjusted. Stated schematically, the criterion of ontic content for specific objects becomes:

6. *s* assumes that $(\exists x)(x = a)$ if and only if *s* implies '$(\exists x)(x = a)$'

Thus the modal expressions and subjunctive give way to implication.[36]

The intent of 6 is clear, but the notation is unsatisfactory. First, '$(\exists x)(x = a)$' is a schema, and will not be implied by any statement or set of statements whereas the wording in the criterion requires that it be so implied. Second, the replacements for '*a*' in the two places are not, strictly speaking the same unless the metalanguage contains the object language; in the first part of the criterion '*a*' is replaceable by a metalinguistic singular term purporting to name a (frequently nonlinguistic) entity, whereas the '*a*' within the quotation in the second part can be replaced only by the singular term in the object language purporting to name the same entity.

Matters may be set right, however by two conventions. First, it is stipulated that the metalanguage used in the criterion will have the object language as a part. Rarely would one wish to *apply* the criterion otherwise, so this restriction involves no loss of practical importance. Second, special quotation marks—they may be called "slipped quotes"—will be used:

7. ‹$(\exists x)(x = a)$.›

Whereas:

'$(\exists x)(x = a)$'

is a name of a specific schema, 7 is a schematic name for sentences of the object language. Replacement of '*a*' in 7 by the singular term of the object language '2' yields:

'$(\exists x)(x = 2)$',

a name of a statement. Thus 7 is simply preserving within quotations, the schematic character of the letter '*a*'. Similarly,

8. ‹ $(\exists x)Fx$ ›

is to be a schematic name of object language sentences. Replacement of '*F*' in 8 by a predicate yields a name of the sentence obtained by replacing '*F*' in the schema '$(\exists x)Fx$' by that predicate.

Using slipped quotes,[37] the criterion of ontic content for specific objects becomes:

9. *s* assumes that $(\exists x)(x = a)$ if and only if *s* implies ‹$(\exists x)(x = a)$›.

And the version for objects of a given kind becomes:

10. *s* assumes that $(\exists x)Fx$ if and only if *s* implies ‹$(\exists x)Fx$.›

The schematic character of these formulations makes them easy to apply. Furthermore they seem generally satisfactory for the purposes for which they were wanted. And they make clear one important point made by Quine: it is through existential quantifications that ontic content is revealed.

(The word 'implies' may be understood differently according to the way in which singular inference is treated. Rather than make any particular treatment an integral part of the criterion of ontic content, it seems better to leave the question open, and to acknowledge that we have a group of criteria. This is not, I think, Quine's view; for him the Quine-Russell approach is integral to the criterion. Furthermore in the rest of this paper we shall use the Quine-Russell rules of elimination along with the criterion.)

To test formulations 9 and 10 of the criterion, we may ask a fifth question: *What statements of ontic content are obtained in applications?* According to the criterion, the following are true (the right-hand parts of the biconditionals being false): [38]

'$(\exists x)(x$ is-red)' does not assume that there is redness,

'$(\exists x)(x$ is-red)' does not assume that there exists the proposition that something is red,

'$\sim(\exists x)(x = $ Pegasus)' does not assume that Pegasus exists. These examples conform with important points in Quine's ontological discussions: No statement itself assumes the existence of properties corresponding to the predicates occurring in it; no statement assumes the existence of the proposition which, some like to say, it expresses; some statements in which singular terms occur do not assume the existence of designata for those terms. It may be added that no statement assumes the existence of classes as extensions of the predicates occurring in it. In some cases predicates occurring within abstracts would be an exception.

Examples involving inconsistent and valid sentences, though of little interest in themselves, frequently provide good tests of theory. The formulations 9 and 10 meet no objections in these cases. It turns out that all and only inconsistent statements assume the existence of $(\imath x)(x$ is an atom $\cdot \sim(x$ is an atom$))$, and that all and only inconsistent statements assume that there are entities which are both atoms and not atoms. If a statement or set of statements assumes that there exists $(\imath x)(x$ is an atom $\text{v} \sim(x$ is an atom$))$, then it implies that there is exactly one entity—a more extreme form of monism than any consistent doctrine ever held. (Most monisms apparently assume the existence of many more than one entity; Quine's criterion of ontic content is helpful in showing this.) Every statement and set of statements assumes that there are entities which are either atoms or not atoms, and entities which are self-identical. Since, whatever implies a statement of the form '$(\exists x)(\exists y)\ Fxy$' will also imply the corresponding statement of the form '$(\exists y)(\exists x)Fxy$', a statement combining a "simple" two-place predicate[39] with two singular terms will assume the existence of designata for both terms.

In any specific instance, the right-hand portion of the biconditional, affirming an implication, is referentially opaque, and consistency requires that the left-hand portion also be construed as opaque. The following statements of ontic content are true:

'$(\exists x)(x = $ Morning Star$)$' assumes the existence of the Morning Star

'$(\exists x)(x = $ Morning Star$)$' does not assume that the Evening Star exists

'$(\exists x)(x = $ Evening Star$)$' assumes that the Evening Star exists

'$(\exists x)(x = $ Evening Star$)$' does not assume the existence of the Morning Star.

The sixth question is: *What happens when the criterion is applied to statements of ontic content?* Does the true statement:

11. '$(\exists x)(x = $ Pegasus$)$' assumes that there exists Pegasus assume that Pegasus exists? Initially, it might appear that, using

the Quine-Russell rule for eliminating singular terms, (11) can be transformed into:

12. $(\exists y)('(\exists x) (x = \text{Pegasus})'$ assumes that there exists y $\cdot y = \text{Pegasus} \cdot (x)(x = \text{Pegasus} \supset x = y))$.

Obviously this, and hence 11, implies '$(\exists x)(x = \text{Pegasus})$'. The second part of the criterion 9 is satisfied, so, it would seem, 11 assumes that Pegasus exists.

We have, however, noted previously that 11 is a referentially opaque construction; 12 involves quantification into that context, in violation of the rule that "no variable inside an opaque construction is bound by an operator outside." [40] This constitutes a restriction on the elimination of singular terms from positions that are not purely referential, and this restriction was not satisfied in the move from 11 to 12. (On the other hand, if 11 is transformed by confining the elimination of the singular term to the fragment 'there exists Pegasus' the result of applying the criterion is that there is no assumption that Pegasus exists.) Nor will statements having the pattern:

s assumes that $(\exists x)Fx$

assume that there are F. Referential opacity guarantees that statements of ontic content do *not* inherit that content. (If the blank in '$s \ldots a$' is filled by a genuine two-place predicate, instances of the result are subject to the argument of the preceding paragraph, and do assume the existence of the entities whose names replace 'a'.)

That statements of ontic content do *not* themselves have that content is a highly desirable result, for one of the purposes for the "semantic ascent" from questions of what is to questions of what a discourse *says* there is was to achieve an ontologically neutral stance which will permit opponents in an ontological controversy to continue their discussions.[41] Referential opacity appears necessary to achieve that neutral position.

The discussion of the first question led to the conclusion that Quine's criterion of ontic commitment is a criterion of ontic content, and is not a matter of pragmatics. Yet, as has been noted, the language used is frequently inescapably pragmatic in character, and there remains an aspect of the matter which has not been taken into account. So our seventh question is: *What is the pragmatic principle of ontic commitment?* It may be noted that the word 'commitment' suggests not only something is pragmatics, but also something vaguely ethical. To make this point clear and explicit, the principle may be worded using 'should' in lieu of 'commit.' Intuitively the principle (in normative pragmatics) of ontic commitment is 'Anyone who accepts a statement or set of statements should also accept its ontic content—i.e., should also accept the existential quantifications stating its content'. But the *fact* of acceptance is not sufficient justification for accepting these quantifications. In some cases statements are actually accepted without proper reasons when there are excellent reasons for rejecting an implied quantification. A better formulation is 'A person either should accept both a statement or a set of statements and the quantifications stating its ontic content or he should not accept the statement or set of statements'.[42] The rule, combined with the criterion of ontic content, amounts to a special case of the command, 'Be consistent', but it invites attention to implications that are too often overlooked.

Notes

1. Willard Van Orman Quine, "Existence and Quantification," in *Ontological Relativity and Other Essays* (New York: Columbia University Press, 1969), p. 96; and "Replies" in Donald Davidson and Jaako Hintikka, eds., *Words and Objections: Essays on the Work of W. V. Quine* (Dordrecht: D. Reidel, 1969), p. 315.

2. Letters quoted in Rudolf Carnap, *Meaning and Necessity* (Chicago: University of Chicago Press, 1956), p. 196.

3. "A Logistical Approach to the Ontological Problem," in *The Ways of Paradox and Other Essays* (New York: Random House, 1966), p. 66.

4. Willard Van Orman Quine, *The Journal of Philosophy* 40 (1943): 118.

5. Willard Van Orman Quine, *From a Logical Point of View*, 2nd ed. rev. (New York: Harper, 1961), p. 13.

6. Ibid., pp. 13–14.

7. *Methods of Logic*, rev. ed. (New York: Holt, 1959), p. 224.

8. *Philosophical Studies* 2 (1951): 11.

9. Ibid., p. 13.

10. *From a Logical Point of View*, 1st ed. (Cambridge: Harvard University Press, 1953), p. 103.

11. 2nd ed. rev., p. 103.

12. Ibid., p. 131.

13. *Ontological Relativity and other Essays*, p. 93.

14. Frederic B. Fitch, review of the 2nd edition of *From a Logical Point of View, Journal of Symbolic Logic* 33 (1968): 149.

15. *From a Logical Point of View*, p. 8.

16. William P. Alston, "Ontological Commitments," *Philosophical Studies* 2 (1958): 12.

17. *From a Logical Point of View*, p. 15.

18. Ibid., p. 103.

19. Ibid., pp. 130–131.

20. Davidson and Hintikka, p. 309.

21. *Ontological Relativity and Other Essays*, p. 51.

22. Quine uses the term 'ontic content' in *Word and Object*, p. 242: "To paraphrase a sentence into the canonical notation of quantification is first and foremost, to make its ontic content explicit."

23. *Ontological Relativity and Other Essays*, p. 51.

24. Applications to *sets* of statements as well as to single statements allows discussion of ontic content in cases such as the infinite set of axioms of Quine's system ML.

25. Yehoshua Bar-Hillel, review of Quine's "Semantics and Abstract Objects" and of Max Black's "Comments" on Quine's paper, *Journal of Symbolic Logic* 17 (1952): 136–137.

26. Review of *From a Logical Point of View*, p. 149.

27. The argument will not hold for theories of singular inference in which terms which designate nothing else designate the null class.

28. Willard Van Orman Quine, *Word and Object* (Cambridge: Technology Press of the Massachusetts Institute of Technology, 1960), pp. 144, 151.

29. Ibid., p. 142.

30. A third alternative would avoid indirect discourse and construe 'assumes' as a two-place predicate relating statements and sets of statements to existential quantifications.

31. 1 is, of course, a special case of 2, but it is of sufficient interest that it may be useful to distinguish cases of 1 from the other cases.

32. *Ontological Relativity and Other Essays*, p. 93.

33. *From a Logical Point of View*, p. 13.

34. Ibid., p. 13–14.

35. *Methods of Logic*, p. 224. The "elliptical" formulation from "A Logistical Approach to the Ontological Problem" involves neither subjunctives nor modalities, but reformulation to avoid the pragmatic element would, perhaps, invite their use. There is one clear statement of the criterion (as applied to existential quantifications) which employs neither subjunctives nor modalities—the one quoted from "Notes on the Theory of Reference." Richard L. Cartwright has, however, shown that this formulation is not satisfactory in "Ontology and the Theory of Meaning," *Philosophy of Science* 21 (1954): 316–325.

36. Fitch in his review of *From a Logical Point of View* suggested explication of the modalities as logical necessity, but did not pursue the point.

37. Slipped quotes appear only in the formulations of the criterion; they do not appear in specific instances of it.

38. Perhaps some theoretical reservations concerning nonimplications

are appropriate. Cf. James Willard Oliver, "Formal Fallacies and Other Invalid Arguments," *Mind* 76 (1967): 463–478. These reservations have nothing to do with the question of whether logic is a "complete and perfect science" (ibid., p. 467)—the writer's view has changed on this point. Some device providing for formal recognition of the "independence" of predicates seems needed.

39. *Methods of Logic*, p. 221.

40. *Word and Object*, p. 166.

41. *From a Logical Point of View*, p. 1.

42. The formulation obviously involves quantification over modalities. I know of no way to eliminate such quantification, and yet it seems important to be able to state such epistemological rules.

RESPONSE

James F. Harris, Jr.

Professor Oliver has raised some interesting and important questions concerning Willard Van Orman Quine's criterion of ontological commitment and has also provided us with some interesting answers. Space permits me to comment only on those questions which I take to be the most important and to briefly raise some additional questions of my own.

Is the criterion an assertion in pragmatics or is the criterion to be regarded as belonging to semantics (p. 94)? Quine's use of phrases like "is committed to," "commits us to the acceptance of," "presupposes," and "assumes" supports an interpretation in pragmatics, Oliver suggests; however, Oliver comes down on the side of semantics. I want to suggest that Quine is consistently ambiguous on this point and that the question is undecidable, and since the case has been made by Oliver for the semantics side, I shall take the side of pragmatics.

As Oliver suggests, Quine calls his well-known aphorism, "To be is to be the value of a variable" a "semantical rule" in "On What There Is," but he does this while treating the question of adjudicating among rival ontologies. Treating such a question on a semantical level has certain desirable practical consequences, Quine says. First, it helps the proponent of the negative side of any argument about the existence of *x* by solving the Platonic problem of nonbeing, and secondly, it provides a common ground upon which opponents can argue.

However, Quine is quick to point out that "we must not jump to the conclusion that what there is depends on words. Translatability of a question into semantical terms is no indication that the question is linguistic." [1] On the contrary, which ontology a person accepts is tied in with what scientific theory—what conceptual scheme—a person accepts which is certainly a pragmatic consideration. So, Quine says, "To whatever extent the adoption of any system of scientific theory may be said to be a matter of language, the same—but no more—may be said of the adoption of an ontology." [2] Quine's use of "semantical formula" does not then appear to be decisive for answering question one.

Oliver suggests that there is a progression in Quine's development of his criterion from the early, pragmatic sounding formulations beginning with the earliest (1939) formulation in "A Logistical Approach to the Ontological Problem" to the more recent formulations which do not use the pragmatic sounding words "commit" and "assume." Such does not appear to be the case. For example, immediately following the early, pragmatic sounding formulation in "A Logistical Approach to the Ontological Problem," "We may be said to countenance such and such an entity if and only if we regard the range of our variables as including such an entity," [3] comes the famed, "To *be* is to be the value of a variable." And even as late as the second edition of *From a Logical Point of View* (1961) Quine is still asking, "Does *nothing* we may say *commit us to the assumption* (italics mine) of universals or other entities which we may find unwelcome?" [4] And he is still saying, "We can very easily involve ourselves in ontological commitments by saying, for example, that *there is something* (bound variable) which red houses and sunsets have in common; or that *there is something* which is a prime number larger than a million. But this is, essentially, the *only* way we can involve ourselves in ontological commitments: by our use of bound variables." [5]

There is at least enough ambiguity in Quine to make William P. Alston regard his pragmatic formulation, "One is ontologically committed to *P*'s if and only if he is unable to say what he wants to say without using a sentence of the form 'There is (are) a *P* ...,' [6] as "substantially equivalent" to Quine's.

Perhaps Quine's ambiguity in this regard was caused by a genuine uncertainty as to whether the criterion *ought* to be in pragmatics or not. Quine often uses "true," "false," "affirmation," etc. even in the more semantical sounding formulations of the criterion. P. F. Strawson's distinctions regarding sentence, use of a sentence, and utterance of a sentence[7] bring to light the issue involved here. If we consider the example, "The King of France is wise," we can easily imagine many different people uttering this sentence at many different times. We might regard one occasion of the *use* of this sentence as true (say, an utterance of the sentence during the reign of Louis XIV) while we would regard another *use* of the sentence as false (say, an utterance of the sentence during the reign of Louis XV). Strawson claims that "Meaning . . . is a function of the sentence or expression; mentioning and referring and truth and falsity, are functions of the use of the sentence or expression." [8] And again, Strawson says, " 'Mentioning', or 'referring', is not something an expression does; it is something that someone can use an expression to do. Mentioning, or referring to, [*sic*] something is a characteristic of *a use* of an expression, just as 'being about' something, and truth-or-falsity, are characteristics of *a use* of a sentence." [9] *Perhaps* Quine may have used "discourse" in the passage Oliver cites from "Logic and the Reification of Universals" in a way which would not be inconsistent with Strawson. Quine says, "The parent who tells the Cinderella story is no more committed to admitting a fairy godmother and a pumpkin coach into his own ontology than to admitting the story as true." [10] A person need not be committed to something (as Oliver suggests) in order for Quine's criterion to be in pragmatics; Quine's concern with the circumstances surrounding the *use* of a sentence—a person's intentions, his seriousness or frivolity—suggests a possible interpretation in pragmatics.

What is the structure of the fragments of the criterion in which "*assumes*" *occurs* (p. 96)? I agree generally with the analysis which follows from Professor Oliver's initial assumptions about the nature of the word "assumes," but I wish to raise a question regarding the assumption that the extension of "assumes," taken as a two-place predicate, " . . . is a relation comprising pairs of statements (and sets of statements and objects). . . ." Oliver's discussion of "assumes" is really a discussion about this assumption, and he decides that "assumes" cannot be a two-place relation holding between statements or sets of statements and entities. There is no attempt to explicate "assumes" itself in terms of implication or some other logical concept. I am not suggesting that such an attempted explication would or would not work; I am simply pointing to the fact that "assumes' is left unexplicated.

The earlier discussion regarding the use of a sentence suggests an interpretation of "assumes" where the relation is between a person's use of a sentence *S*, and the circumstances which make that particular use of the sentence *S*, appropriate. In the case of assertive sentences these circumstances will often include the actual existence of entities, but not always. For example, suppose Sir Edmund Hillary says to the Geological Society of London in a formal lecture on the first expedition to the top of Mt. Everest, "I've been to the mountain top." Hillary's use of the sentence assumes (or "presupposes" appears to be a better word) the existence of a mountain to whose top he has been. However, the circumstances surrounding Dr. Martin Luther King, Jr.'s utterance "I've been to the mountain top," appear quite different, and his use does not appear to assume the existence of a mountain to whose top King has been. Distinguishing between these two uses of a sentence seems entirely appropriate to me. "Assumes" then can be explicated as the relationship between the use of a sentence *s*, and the circumstances which prevent that use of *s*, from being false, void, or to use J. L. Austin's generic word "infelicitous."

What statements of ontic content are obtained in applications (p. 100)? Oliver's use of '$(\exists x)$ (*x* is red)' and of '$(\exists x)$ ($x =$ Morning Star), reflects a shift in Quine's criterion of which nothing has been said. '$(\exists x)$ (x is red) assumes that there is redness' is false, but '$(\exists x)$ (x = Morning Star) assumes the existence of the Morning Star' is true. The difference can only be accounted for by the different interpretations of 'is'. To be is no longer to be the value of a variable; it is the 'is identical with' interpretation of 'is' which does the committing. This point is implicit when Oliver mentions Quine's point that "No statement itself assumes the existence of properties corresponding to the predicate occurring in it. . . ." Paraphrased, this simply means that the predicative sense of 'is' does not result in ontological commitment.

Oliver's use of hyphens in

'$(\exists x)$ (*x* is-red)' does not assume that there is redness, and in

'($\exists x$) (x is-red)' does not assume that there exists the proposition that something is red

does not appear to me to help in this regard. Indeed, the use of such a notational device seems to really draw greater attention to the different meanings of 'is'—one to relate properties to the subject in a predicative sense, and the other to relate a predicate nominative to the subject in a relation of identity.

What is the pragmatic principle of ontic commitment (p. 102)? My interest in this question should be evident by my comments concerning question one. I agree with Professor Oliver's comments here, and I think that this is what Austin had in mind when he compared 'All John's children are bald but John hasn't got any children' to 'I promise to but I don't intend to'. Although neither of these involves an explicit contradiction, I agree that one should feel outrage at being told such. The difficulty is not logical (at least not in a strict sense), and calling the obligation which a person is under not to utter such statements a *normative* obligation captures well, I think, the nature of the problem. This is a consideration which certainly invites and deserves further attention.

Finally, there are some questions which unfortunately can only be asked here, but which seem to strike even more deeply at the roots of Quine's criterion of ontological commitment.

Granted that linguistic reference is the paradigm way or the only way of making ontological commitments, why are assertions given such a special status? 'Close the door, please' seems to commit the speaker to an open door in much the same way as 'There is an open door' does. Part of Austin's significance to philosophy lies in his observation that "when we state something . . . we . . . perform an act which every bit is as much an act as an act of ordering or warning. There seems to be no good reason why stating should be given a specially unique position." [12] Austin may be wrong in suggesting that we need to take assertion down from the pedestal on which it has been placed, but at any rate, the question must be considered.

The question specifically arises with respect to Oliver's statement 6. Why must s name only an assertion and not other sentences? 'Close the door, please' appears to assume the existence of an open door even though it cannot strictly imply such since it is not an assertion.

Is Quine's criterion a criterion for ontological commitment generally or ontological commitment for some particular language

L_o? The answer seems to be definitely the latter (only for "theories" in quantificational form or reducible to that form), but as Quine has suggested about analyticity,[13] must we not understand the general term 'ontologically committed to'? Must we not understand 'L is ontologically committed to O' where 'L' and 'O' are variables since Quine himself has shown that quantification form is eliminable? Quine's criterion might be viewed as simply the *application* within a particular language L, of a *general* criterion.

Notes

1. Willard Van Ormand Quine, *From a Logical Point of View*, 2nd ed. rev. (New York: Harper and Row, 1961), p. 16.

2. Ibid., p. 17.

3. Willard Van Orman Quine, "A Logistical Approach to the Ontological Problem," in *The Ways of Paradox and Other Essays* (New York: Random House, 1966), p. 66.

4. *From a Logical Point of View*, p. 12.

5. Ibid.

6. William P. Alston, "Ontological Commitments," *Philosophical Studies* 9 (1958): 12.

7. P. F. Strawson, "On Referrıng," *Mind*, 1950. (Page numbers refer to reprint in Charles E. Caton, *Philosophy and Ordinary Language* (University of Illinois Press, 1963), p. 168ff. That account follows Strawson's very closely.

8. Ibid., p. 171.

9. Ibid., p. 170.

10. Quine, *From a Logical Point of View*, p. 103.

11. J. L. Austin, "Performative Utterances," in *Philosophical Papers*, ed. J. O. Urmson and G. J. Warnock (Oxford University Press, 1961), pp. 235–236.

12. Ibid., p. 236.

13. Quine, *From a Logical Point of View*, p. 33.

EVENTS AND PAST EVENTS: SOME ONTOLOGICAL CONSIDERATIONS

L. B. Cebik

It cannot have escaped anyone's notice that there are events in the world as well as things—George Boas.

The philosophy of history harbors a classic debate which, amidst the talk of Caesar crossing the Rubicon and Richard losing both horse and kingdom, hides something relevant to ontology. The most general lines of disagreement appear in the charge often leveled against idealists such as Collingwood: They reduce the past to what the historian makes it. To the contrary, so the argument periodically goes, only because there is "history as actuality" can there be written history. The one denies what the other affirms: that there is a distinction to be made between what historians deal in and what happened.

The debate is more illusory than real. It arises, as I shall take some time to show, from misconceptions concerning event concepts, the central misconception being the attempt to apply portions of the logic of object language to event language.[1] It will not do, nonetheless, merely to deny the misconception, for rarely do theorists affirm it. Instead, when the philosophic going gets tough, they lapse into object language, and their lapses must be weeded out one at a time. I shall weed only a few.

Ontological questions enter from the very beginning. In brief, events turn out not to be the sorts of "things" to have ontological status. And the usual distinction between written and actual history, paralleling as it does the distinction between a word and the object to which it refers, turns out to be illicit. History and the philosophy thereof have always been the disreputable cousins to traditional philosophic concerns precisely because the former deal almost wholly in events while the latter have built about themselves a fabric of object relevant categories. Little wonder, then, that attempts to integrate conceptual studies of event concepts into more established philosophic doctrines have foundered badly. Even the most expressive metaphors, such as trying to put square pegs into round holes, betray an inexorable prejudice.

I

Theorists have not quarrelled with the possibility of written history, a past expressed in language, full of interpretation, resting on evidence, and subject to revision according to new evidence or interpretation. That much of a past, that created and/or discovered by the historian, seems acceptable to all disputants, perhaps because it is the past for which library books supply a ready referent when the words "history" and "past" are used.

Debate, however, arises in connection with the past, the history, the collection of events which history books, documents, and other materials are supposed to be about. The idealists, for example, found strong reason to disavow such a past. Oakeshott denounced the notion, especially as it implied a "fixed and finished past, a past independent of present experience, . . . a past divorced from and uninfluenced by the present . . . . " [2] Such a past, argues Oakeshott, "is a past divorced from evidence (for evidence is always present) and is consequently nothing and unknowable." Thus, there are not two worlds, one of present experience and one of past happenings, but instead only one world: a present world of ideas in which the past is no more than an inference.[3]

An event's being past is a function of "a special organization" of the present. Oakeshott's expression for history, "what the evidence obliges us to believe," functions almost as a name for that special organization: the categories, chronologies, and inferences which history by nature involves.

Oakeshott's argument does more than deny that one may assert the present existence of past events; it also insists that the assertion of the past existence of past events is wholly an historical assertion. Thus, the past—events as they really were—is not only impossible to know, but immaterial to history. Past events are not the objects of historical study; they are products of historical research and construction.

Collingwood echoes the arguments of his fellow Briton against the past, against "events that have finished happening." [14] Past events neither exist nor are perceivable; our knowledge of them is not subject to verification by experiment. Rather, presently existing "evidence (or data)" and principles of interpretation permit inference to the occurrence of past events. If "what really happened" means anything but "what the evidence indicates," e.g., a "real past," then the phrase functions only to set a limit for historical knowledge; it represents "the thing-in-itself . . . , not only unknown but unknowable, not only unknowable but nonexistent." [5]

Although naturalism and historical realism have given implied consent, affirmation of the reality and existence of the past does not necessarily chain one to a naive empiricism.[6] To choose an example who hovers above the chasm between the idealists and empiricists, Beard affirms the past as real and existent, though uncapturable. "History as past actuality" comprises "all that has been done, said, felt, and thought by human beings on this planet since humanity began its long career." [7] To actuality, Beard contrasts "history as record," the evidence, the documents and relics which enable knowledge about history as past actuality, and "history as thought," thought about history as past actuality, "instructed and delimited by history as record and knowledge . . . , authenticated by criticism and ordered with the help of the scientific method." [8]

No matter how massive the attempt, no one can capture the whole of history as actuality. Moreover, the captured pieces result from a "selection and arrangement of facts," acts of "choice, conviction, and interpretation respecting values." [9] The particular choice may prove a fit subject for psychology, but that one chooses by reference to values is endemic to human thought. More importantly, that one must choose is a necessary feature of doing history.

Much more can be done with Beard's views, and Danto does it. Lauding Beard for recognizing the ordinary but correct distinctions among historics, he tightens the relations among them. Insofar as "history as record" serves as evidence for "history as actuality," the former presupposes the latter.[10] "To count something as *evidence* is already to be making a statement about something else, namely, that for which it is taken as evidence." One does not move from "history as record" to "history as actuality"; instead, "just to be seeing something as 'history as record' is already to have made that move." [11] The evidential nature of historical activity is not a contingent fact, but logically necessary and built into the language itself. For example, the use of past-referring predicates, such as "scar," "presupposes that things in the present have had causes in the past," such as wounds.[12] "We automatically acquire our concept of a past as we acquire a language." [13]

The doing of history proceeds via "overarching" conceptions which go beyond description and which make impossible the ideal of history "as an imitation or duplication of the past." [14] Possible, without a priori limit, are any number of temporal structures making reference to discontinuous events which might include among their number a given event, E, and hence also possible are any number of narrative sentences, "each of which truly describes" E. The end product of doing history is thus not a reproduction of "history as actuality," but a narrative, a story built upon evidence and some "organizing scheme" arising from "specific human interests." [15]

Oddly enough, Danto's extension of Beard's "ordinary" distinctions produces a view of the historical discipline which bears striking similarities to Collingwood's. The historian does not seek to reproduce the past, nor is he forced by limitations of space and time to select out of the past those events he will relate. History consists in telling stories, constructing narratives according to some organizing scheme, some human interest, some question in need of answer.[16] The tale one tells is built upon what the evidence allows one to say. Where gaps exist, the historian fills them with what Danto calls "conceptual evidence" or what Collingwood terms interpolative "constructive history" with its source in "the historical imagination." [17] Allowing for the differing jargon stemming from separable philosophic traditions, there is a more than coincidental similarity between Danto's claim that the notion of the past is acquired with language and Collingwood's avowal that the "idea of history" is "in Cartesian language, innate; in Kantian language, a priori." [18]

Nonetheless, and for all the coincidence of their explications of written history, the two differ on the essential issue of the existence of history as actuality, of the past. Collingwood holds history as actuality to be unknown, unknowable, and nonexistent, while Danto takes its existence to be necessarily presupposed in the very concepts which undergird the historian's work.

2

The long-standing debate over past events is part of a larger problem concerning the nature of event concepts. What has not been seriously entertained as a possibility worth exploring is that perhaps event assertions require a different analysis as a starting point to the solution of the traditional philosophic problems which surround events. Indeed, such an analysis is a necessary step in making good the claim that the issue of the existence of past events and the past is illicit and the result of introducing at various points inappropriate elements of object language analysis. If one is to ask intelligibly if there is or can be an existent past, one must take the necessary first step and understand what it is to say an event occurred.

One might ordinarily be tempted to begin an account of event concepts by saying, "let E be an event." Danto, for example, does that sort of thing.[19] Such a formulation allows one to go on to speak of describing E, of making an assertion about E, of redescribing E. The last phrase in particular engenders the claim that there are no limits to the possible descriptions of an event.

The difficulty with such a formulation is that it presupposes one understands what "E" stands for or refers to and what E's are in general. Paul Weiss, for instance, in unashamed metaphysical wonder tells us that an event has at least two moments, that an event is something having a beginning and ending.[20] That, of course, will not do. Every historian knows the futility of seeking termini for the French Revolution or the Renaissance. We can *give* termini, but they do not constitute essential characteristics of events *in general*.

The attempt to treat events as having characteristics is one example of the temptation to treat events according to canons of object language. It comprises part of the larger problem denoted by letting "E" stand for an event. Without specification in terms of a particular kind of event—a specification involving the use of an event concept—"E" stands for nothing at all. To let "E" stand for an event is to mislead through the suggestion that there are certain characteristics essential to events.

One cannot solve the problem by letting "E" stand for some spatiotemporal complex. For such complexes are not events. Events may occur within a complex, or they may mark the move from one complex to another. One may, for example, call the activity of Copernicus the discovery of heliocentric theory or the rediscovery of that theory.[21] One may also call it the writing of a book, the entertaining of heretical thoughts, and so on. But a caution must be placed upon the notion of "calling the activity." In the present context, the phrase locates a so-called spatiotemporal complex, but it does not name a something called an activity or even an event. Not everything in the complex is involved in each assertion, although the "materials" of the complex, the objects, events, actions, et al., permit each of the assertions (except, of course, the assertion of rediscovery, which makes necessary reference outside the boundaries marked out).

One of the central assertions of those who affirm the existence of "history as actuality" is that historians do not reproduce that history. Every description of E is from a point of view and for a purpose, and there is no limit to the possible redescriptions of E. Danto goes so far as to suggest "rules of redescription." Any argument in favor of such a notion, however, presupposes that "E" denotes something for the description to be of. Notes Danto, "phenomena *as such* are not explained. It is only phenomena as covered by a description which are capable of explanation." [22] Although Danto is correct to relate explanation to the concepts in terms of which one asserts the occurrence of an event, he is incorrect to suppose there are two things: the event/phenomenon/action and the event/phenomenon/action covered by a description.

The feature of language called description only furthers the illusion that event concepts have referents. The cop asks witnesses, "What happened?" (for "something" surely happened). A replies, "There was a tragic accident." B says, "The black sedan ran a red light." C offers, "A lot of good metal turned into scrap." One is tempted to say that they all saw the same thing, as if "the same thing" carried the force it has when A says, "I see the pigskin," and B notes, "I see the inflated, egg-shaped, leather-covered ball," and C remarks, "I see the football." Popular accounts lay any difference between kinds of cases to the complexity of the first, or they put the problem of witnessing events, like beauty, in the more than metaphorical eye of the beholder. In the case of objects, however, for all three to be said to have seen the same thing, there must be one or more identifiable features common to the perception of all the speakers. That is, "inflated, egg-shaped, leather-covered ball," "football," and "pigskin" are analytically related for the given context. However, the cop's problem is that running a red light, turning metal into scrap, and being a tragic accident are not analytically related. There is no central object having definable qualities such that the notion of "analyticity" (or its correlate "syntheticity") finds application.[23]

The point of the example is to reveal a certain peculiarity of events with contrast to objects. The twin notions of reference and description apply to events only after some assertion of a particular event's occurrence has been made. Once one has said, "An accident occurred at Main and Broad," then one can refer to the accident and describe it (It was tragic). Prior to the original assertion, the common request to *describe* what happened amounts only to the request to tell or say what happened, i.e., it is a request for the assertion of an event. Descriptions and references applicable to one event, of course, may not be applicable to another; descriptions applicable to the accident may not be applicable to running a red light.

Is the accident, then, a different event from running the red light? Are they the same event? Or parts of an event? Or perspectives on an event? Such questions contain traps for the issue, for they take attention away from the logic of event concepts and provide seemingly phenomenal levers upon which to raise the question to metaphysical heights.[24] Running a red light and turning metal into scrap may be said to refer to the same accident in a suit brought to court by an insurance company. In traffic court, where the question might be to determine a traffic violation and responsibility for the accident, talk of scrap metal might be relevantly disallowed: the concern is for the accident and its causes, not its results. The notions, thus, of "same" and "different," of "whole" and "part," of "perspective" derive their sense and applicability from the context within which and purpose for which questions and statements occasioning their use might arise. Put another way, there is nothing prior to the assertion of an event to provide the necessary constancy of reference that would give grounds for the notation "E" or univocal meanings for "same," "different," etc.

The desired constancy of reference which theorists desire for events in order to account for the many possible descriptive assertions is often imported via objects. In order to call a discovery by Copernicus a rediscovery, and to call one a redescription of the other, Danto moves from treating the relevant terms as event concepts and takes them to be describing a common object, Copernicus' theory. In many instances, such a maneuver is possible and proper with respect to using language, but it contributes nothing to the understanding of event concepts when taken in itself to explain or to slide by an explanation of event concepts. Danto succeeds only in redescribing an object, the theory, as discovered and rediscovered, instead of redescribing events. Nor need we always resort to objects to obtain the desired constancy of reference. In speaking of events, one does not say everything, but only everything relevant to the purpose for which speaking of events is initiated. Within such a frame of reference, one can determine not only the propriety of what is said about particular events, but also the propriety of mentioning particular events. Thus, it is possible to circumscribe that about which one is talking without resorting to objects. Supplying a referent will not substitute for an analysis of event concepts on their own grounds.

3

The use of event concepts does not depend upon there being an object or a something capable of having qualities, the presence of which warrants a certain description which definitionally equals a certain object word. More simply, the use of event concepts depends in no way upon preassertorial reference.

Rather, as I have argued elsewhere,[25] the use of event concepts is warranted by the fulfillment of criteria. It may be, and has been argued that object concepts are also warranted in use by criteria fulfillment.[26] However, the use and the logical analysis of object concepts can be held to be separable.[27] The same cannot be said for event concepts, which, since they are not amenable to the referent-description distinction, leave for analysis only their criteria of application. One result of this fact is that to assert the occurrence of an event and to use warrantably an event concept must be taken to be the same thing. The justification of the assertion and the justification of the use are identical: that certain criteria may be said to be fulfilled, where those criteria might be physical features, behavior, other events, objects, or any number of other items.

Treating event concepts in this manner eliminates numerous problems left by previous analyses. For example, is an event, like the Renaissance, related to other events, like da Vinci painting the *Mona Lisa*, as whole to part, as class to member, as extension increase or decrease to an appropriate change of intension? Rickert had viewed event concepts (historical concepts) as increasing in extension with increases in intension. Nagel attempted to solve this logically embarrassing situation by taking the range of events, entities, et al., covered by an event concept such as "Renaissance," to be parts comprising an historical whole.[28] Dray, in part, treats historical concepts as classificatory such that a group of events "amounts" to a larger scale event "Q," without need or addition of further empirical information.[29]

All these schemes, however, suffer the same root fault of attempting to apply object language categories to events. Intension and extension are simply irrelevant. Da Vinci's painting the *Mona Lisa* or the work itself are not in any straightforward way referred to by the term "Italian Renaissance." Either may be used as an *example* of the sort of thing that went on to warrant calling the period renaissant in the arts, but no single work or act is necessarily referred to by the term, nor would any single work or act warrant the term. Da Vinci's work is part of the Renaissance by virtue of being a criteria-fulfilling event, whereas da Vinci's eating spaghetti is not such a part, though the event occurs during or within the Renaissance. Thus, the notion of whole-part in this connection cannot be taken as like that applied to objects, wherein no part can be rejected. The multi-utility of the notion of whole-part permits the illusion of similarity, and a comparable illusion arises with classification. To the extent that a series of events and entities warrant the assertion of event Q, one can say that they are called Q or classified as Q. But, such a use of "classify" should not be confused with the rigid senses in which classes are formed via essential or accidental qualities of the members. With many event concepts, the criterial events and entities need have no common feature, as when a revolution is asserted to have occurred on the basis of an overthrow of a government, institution of a new ruling power, and so on.

With event concepts, then, there is nothing of concern save the criteria to be fulfilled to warrant assertion of the event. Obviously, many assertions are made without explicit justification, and mention of criteria normally occurs only when an assertion is or is called in question. Often questions involve a single crucial event or entity and give rise to the temptation of believing that the single item in question comprises a sufficient ground for the assertion. The next easy step would be to define the questioned concept in terms of the crucial criterion, and the object mode of handling concepts would then have crept back into play. Criteria, of course, are neither qualities nor conditions of events.

The criteria-fulfilling items may be events as well as entities, and wherever they are events, they themselves require criterial justification. This fact alone suffices to account for the tumbling of large scale historical assertions with the correction of but a minor slip. For example, A. J. P. Taylor denied that Hitler masterminded a complete plan of political conquest for Europe, and rested his denial on the fact that whatever plans existed were war college contingency plans which were not political and never used politically.[30] More importantly, whenever a single concept is used, its criteria are presupposed. Suppose "x," "y," and "z" to be criteria for asserting "Q," and further that one asserts 'Q resulted in a reduction of Europe's population'. The assertion presupposes in a straightforward sense that Q occurred. That Q occurred presupposes that criteria "x," "y," and "z" are fulfilled, i.e., that x, y, and z occurred, exist, or are the case, as appropriate. So long as the results of Q are in question, "Q" and its criteria are not, and appropriate circumstances would have to exist in order to provide grounds for questioning "Q" or "x," "y," and "z." To the extent that x, y, and z may be events, the use of an event concept "Q" rests on the supposition of the proper use of other event concepts.

There is, consequently, no fundamental level of events, one to which no further suppositions can be charged. In other words, event concepts cannot be reduced either to a definite set or to a particular kind such that other event suppositions are excluded. Such a possibility is tempting in view of the fact that the examples which come readily to mind are usually "large" historical events—battles, revolutions, plans—whose criteria of justified assertion are "smaller" events—personal conflicts, individual actions, acts which are steps to a goal. Such examples, in part, lie behind certain versions of the suggestion that history can be reduced to a basic narrative.[31] However, such examples do not exhaust the possibilities. To assert that Copernicus *rediscovered* the heliocentric theory is criterially to suppose the correctness of asserting that someone (Aristarchus, perhaps) discovered the heliocentric theory. To assert that John is contemplating, a "mental act," may require justification in terms of gross physical behavior. Is the contemplation "larger" or "smaller" than the behavior? To the extent that the behavior may not even be a component of the contemplation despite its criterial function, the terms "larger," "smaller" and others suggesting possible reductions do not appropriately apply. In general, the relevant distinction to be made remains that between criteria and concept, and there can logically be no prejudice toward any particular sort of concept outside the context of use within which the criteria-concept distinction achieves relevance.

Certain ontological implications of this analysis should be clear. There is no such thing as an event-in-itself and apart from the concepts used to assert the occurrence of events. Nor is there any particular sort of event which has, in general, ontological priority over others. That such notions have occasionally arisen results from the application of object language categories to event concepts. At least four such attempted applications (the common ones, but not all of them) have been noted. One was the attempt to treat events as having characteristics, analogous to objects with predicable qualities or attributes. A second was the attempt to let event concepts denote, as if in question were two separable entities analogous to word and object. A third was the suggested application to event concepts of object-dissection categories: whole-part, class-member, extension-intension, etc. Wherever such notions found warranted use with events, their senses differed radically from that connected with object applications. Fourth was the attempt to find for events a basic level, roughly corresponding to the observable-qualities-of-an-entity level for objects which comprises for much historical metaphysics a dubious starting point. There are undoubtedly other ways in which object categories are overtly or surreptitiously, consciously or unconsciously applied to events, but the four given seem to be the most misleading and obvious. And it can be of but little wonder that misapplied logic should lead to misconceptions and confusions with respect to ontological questions.

4

Events, of course, do not exist. They occur; they happen. Actions also occur, and have agents. Agents perform actions, do acts. At this point, to counter that objects are necessarily involved in events and actions, and they exist, would amount to an evasion, for the question at hand does not concern the present or past existence of objects. Indeed, that one feels no difficulty in saying that objects exist and have existed supplies one source of the problem of events. The point of noting that events do not exist (and, as a corollary, do not *not exist*) is solely to call attention to the applicable concepts for discussing events.

There are events, however, just as much as there are objects. Although the constructions are parallel, theoretical inquiry into what it is for there to be objects and events necessarily results in two quite different questions. For the only means of initially answering the inquiry is in terms of the distinction between existing and occurring. Moreover, the explication of "existence" and "occurrence" cannot consist in laying down a definitional meaning for each of those terms. Such an explication would treat both notions as object concepts. Rather, the terms are logical placeholders; they assert nothing about events or objects, but instead distinguish treatments of two categories of concepts. They signal, at best, how object concepts and event concepts are to be used. In other words, they distinguish the logics of object and event concepts. To say events occur is not to say something general or metaphysical about events; it is to say something about the manner in which event assertions are justified and what sort of implications can be drawn from an event assertion.

Too much can be made of the parallels between object and event constructions. For example, it is legitimate but misleading to note that one can speak both of seeing an object and seeing an event. Something quite different is involved in each of these "seeings." One can go back and take another look at an object without having to resort to instant replay. In general, to express the matter Humeanly, one views the qualities of objects. However, one views events by seeing those things that would warrant the assertion of a particular event. The point of using instant replay would be to see if criteria are fulfilled which warrant an assertion under fire or some further assertion. The pattern of players, the rapid retreat of the passer, the soft pass to the fullback, the wall of blockers together warrant the assertion of a screen pass. In a questionable case, the commentator watches the film to decide if the play was called or simply developed by accident (of the receiver's and blockers' positions) and necessity (due to the blitz of the linebackers). He decides the play was called: a warranted assertion even though he was not privy to the huddle. Yes, one sees events, but like reading, seeing one is no simple, primitive, or unschooled act.

Seeing past events, without instant replay equipment, does not represent a normal way of talking about what one does when one asserts that something happened. However, there is no difference in logical principle between asserting present and asserting past events. Before stadiums were equipped with direct lines to radio stations, baseball games were sometimes indirectly broadcast, with the studio announcer fed a telegraphed running account. Reese at third. Robinson bunts. On his own, the announcer hollers, "It's a squeeze play!" Whether the event is past or still going on when he hollers makes no difference. He has correctly called the play.[32]

When events are far enough past or far enough distant, we move from speaking of criteria to speaking of evidence for the event's occurrence. There exists no hard and fast boundary between evidential and nonevidential assertions of events, although there are desiderata which occasion one use or the other. Import, or the crucialness of deciding whether something happened, is one major factor. The more important the case, the more one wants to evaluate formally the justification for an assertion. Evidence is something evaluateable, and the more formal the procedure, the more explicit the standards, the more self-conscious the method, then the greater the occasion for speaking of evidence. Where events are remote in time or place, and criteria-fulfilling information is concomitantly scarce, one is also inclined to speak of the available information as evidence, especially in cases where assertions contain an element of justificational risk. These factors (and others as well) do not always act in concert: there are cases where the evidence is clear-cut and overwhelming and cases, too, of evidence for trivial matters. Evidential evaluation is not always formal and overt. Still, the point of mentioning these matters is only to loosen a prejudice from event concepts: there is nothing logically special about cases to which one ordinarily applies the term evidence. History, law, criminology, and other fields have special techniques of evidence evaluation, special methodologies, but these are concerned (mostly) with being able to fulfill the criteria for the assertion of an event. Often, their development and use produce alternative and specialized criteria for event assertion, i.e., new uses of event concepts. Nonetheless, the subject of evidence techniques does not speak to or alter the fundamental criterial justification of event concepts themselves.[33]

Danto was essentially correct to note that to refer to something as evidence is to suppose certain theses concerning causality and to take them as built into the language.[34] What can be misleading is the undue theoreticalness contained in his combination of terms, "theses" and "causality." Elsewhere, he minimizes the notion of causality to the Humean contents of succession and contiguity, plus his own addition, change. Even these small requirements, however, lend too much formality to the desired general analysis and place too much weight upon a pseudo-scientific sense of evidence as opposed to the less demanding notion of criteria. There are all manner of inferential connections, each contextually limited, many warranted upon the flimsiest of truisms,[35] and the only grounds at all for calling many of them causal seems to be in order to distinguish them from those which are analytically or deductively grounded. In addition, one would be most likely correct to say that evidential connections are based upon successful past usage, that the results of a process of association are built into the very use of "past-referring expressions." Danto's example—"scar"—is helpful to the extent that, and contrary to his own analysis, it is not a priori possible to say whether the connection—between "scar" and "wound"—is to be analytic or causal in particular cases.[36] Such judgments rest upon the added material of context and upon the point of raising the question.

There are, then, past events in the same sort of way that there are present events, i.e., in that one can assert what is happening or what happened. For such assertions, criteria can be fulfilled regardless of whether the event is near or distant, present or past, and without reducing past assertions to present. What differ are the kinds of criteria-fulfilling items, not the criterial relation. Thus, great restriction must be placed upon Danto's high sounding dictum that history owes its existence to the fact that we have no direct access to the past. All that the want of direct access can mean, given the present account, is that we can no longer send out a reliable witness. But we can find reliable witnesses in history. In the sense of direct access Danto seems to want, seeing for ourselves, we never did have direct access to most of the events historians consider important, e.g., revolutions, wars, depressions, assassinations, etc. To a large degree we lack such direct access to the present, not because such events are invisible or because we are blind or in the wrong place, but rather because "seeing" and allied notions of direct access are inapplicable. That the historian is not forbidden from present battles while the journalist is forbidden from those of the past says less to what history is than to what journalism can do. And what it says is a report, not an explanation.[37]

Moreover, history is not coterminal with the possible body of assertions or true assertions of or about past events, although there is, in principle, no logical difference between the historian's assertions and those of others. (There may, of course, be considerable methodological difference.) The notions of "past history" and "historical events" do not denote something special by way of logic. Rather, they indicate those events and other matters of concern to historians. The confusion of emphasis and interest with intrinsic and essential features has done much to hinder the understanding of history and of the underlying nature of event concepts.

In this section, I have treated history as that body of work done by historians, that series of assertions they make as to what happened, what events occurred. Historians, as noted earlier, go on to make assertions *about* events. To claim that assertions about things can only be made of objects or entities having existence independently of the use of a concept would amount to mere prejudice. For the rules of "about" depend upon grammar, not logic, and "about" applies to any substantive, any noun. Event words are nouns. To make an assertion about an event is nothing special: it is what kinds of things can be said about events that is limited by the logic of events. Events, for example, have features rather than qualities, that is, they have criterial and non-criterial objects, events, and states (where "have" does not indicate possession), rather than functions and observable, predicable attributes. Lots may be said about events, but not the same sorts of things as about objects.

But what about "history's" other major sense, the past itself? What, if anything, may be said about it, and what, if anything, is it? Upon such questions, the answers to which depend upon the analysis so far given, rest the original debate and the closing section of this essay.

5

Many questions may be intended by asking if there is a past, but four major variants appear relevant to the present context.

1. If one means by the question, "have things happened?" the answer is a somewhat trivial yes. However, the import of this version of the question lies with the answer rather than with the grounds for answering, which are simply that we have found out *that* events have occurred by finding out *which* events have taken place. To the extent, then, that the question of the past involves some manner of summation of particular events, it necessarily involves techniques for arriving at assertions of what happened, and thus is coterminal with the means for finding out the past. In no way, therefore, does this interpretation of the question imply or suggest a past differing from that comprising the body of correct historical and other past assertions.

2. In the attempt to give the question broader scope, one may note that history has not asserted all of what it must be possible to assert. What occurred without trace or witness fills the time span between events for which there is evidence. It is the totality of both sorts of events to which "the past" refers. As such, the past is not what history asserts, but something more, if not different, and just this past is ontologically in question.

The argument denies that a special past is intended. What is intended by "the past for which historians have no evidence" is only that something *must* have occurred between the events which history does assert on the basis of evidence. Collingwood suggests something of the sort when he notes that between Caesar being in Gaul and later in Rome he *must* have done something, for which historians have no evidence.[38] The present argument would maintain that the past includes all that Caesar did, not just what historians say he did. However, the assertion that he must have done something is as much an historical assertion as the ones placing Caesar in Gaul and in Rome. Collingwood calls the means for making such assertions "the historical imagination," while Danto refers to the means as "conceptual evidence." [39] The point of their solutions to the matter is to note that assertions about the past (whether or not formally historical) are not limited to the interpretation of *pieces* of evidence, i.e., objects and manuscripts, but include all the logical and conceptual machinery by which statements are ordinarily made. Danto's term may be the better of the two, for it is not imagination that Caesar *journeyed* to Rome from Gaul; rather, it is analytic to the extent that "journey" is the appropriate word to use in expressing the transition of a person from one time and place to a later time and differing place. The choice of "journey" is not analytic to the extent that other possibilities exist: perhaps the drift of his army in pursuit of enemies brought Caesar to Rome without intention. But there is no evidence, where one would expect to find evidence, to support what thus becomes a less plausible account. History, indeed, deals less in the alternatives "true" and "false" and more in the realm of what is more and less plausible. Criteria of assertion provide sufficient grounds for an assertion; they do not provide sufficient grounds for ruling out all other assertions. Consequently, especially where evidence is but questionably sufficient, conflicting (though not contradictory) assertions are often possible. An evaluation and weighing of the evidence, as well as the total story to be told and the purpose of its telling, provide the basic grounds for deciding which of conflicting assertions is the more plausible. To claim that something occurred between well-evidenced events thus comprises part of history's assertion possibilities, and historians give not only what *must* have happened, but their reasons (where not obvious) for so asserting.

    3. A third sort of past to which a theoretician might allude

derives from Collingwood's suggestion that the historian has an a priori "idea" of the past as a whole into which all the pieces developed via evidence fit consistently. Such an a priori whole supplies the form of history, while historians supply the content.[40] The whole is thus a past which is not a part of history and vice versa. While this idea is not the hoped for past which historians can copy, partially grasp, and talk about, it is a separable past, if it is anything at all, and deserves comment.

Whether anyone has such an idea is a moot point. What the idea can be is explicable. The a priori past as a whole is the extension of what is implied by the forms of language used to make past event assertions. A narrative, for example, is a "then and then and then" form of recitation. Beginnings, endings, and breaks are all arbitrary insofar as they are not logically necessitated either by the content—the event assertions themselves—or by the form of the report. Instead, they are chosen with respect to the purpose for and the framework within which the tale is told. Too much and too little equally spoil the story and diminish its point and effect. In short, and beyond narratives, which comprise only a small part of the conceptual tools for making past event assertions, there are no necessary conceptual breaks between event assertions, and there are no logical grounds for denying the possibility of making event assertions such that each abuts or overlaps another without demanding impossible or implausible actions or events and without leaving even a millisecond uneventful. Just such an account is Oakeshott's narrative "with no lacuna," and the conception of history as a complete world of ideas expresses little more than the fact that the language does not preclude completion of the narrative.[41]

Such notions, however, represent formal possibilities of language and not an existent past underlying history.

4. The final noteworthy alternative is the suggestion that the past is simply that: what happened in the past to which the historian has no direct access. His statements may be said (or not) to be about it, but in any event, history works on evidence to say what happened and, in so doing, supposes the actuality of such a past simply by calling his materials evidence. Perhaps this past constitutes that which Danto affirms, and which Collingwood denies on the grounds that such an unknowable "thing-in-itself" is nothing at all.

Arrival at a past which is actual, yet unknowable depends upon straining the ambiguity in the expression "that for which present materials are evidence." To call something evidence and then to note the calling presupposes a past (and even a causal connection to it) is to make a conceptual remark about the form and formulae of past event assertions. The presupposition is not of a set of somethings or others (one cannot say events or occurrences, since that is what historians assert) which once existed but now do not. Neither is the presupposition of a continuum: "continuum" and "set" form a distinction, not a pair of logical complementaries.[42] Rather, the presupposition is of the applicability of those forms of language and logic to which the content of the materials may be fitted in the making of specific past-event assertions. That much of this latest past is logical rather than ontological.

The past for which present materials are evidence is not the past presupposed by calling materials evidence. The past for which present materials are evidence is the purely ordinary past, the eventful past asserted by historians, history itself. This past makes use of the forms of language and logic presupposed by using the term "evidence" (and a host of others as well) but is not identical with the presupposition. It consists in the events for which the evidence is evidence. Indeed, this last seems to be the point of Collingwood's assertion that "evidence is not evidence until it is *used* as evidence." [43] The key word, "used," indicates that the notion of evidence is also logically related to the material results of its employment, the specific assertions of past events which the evidence justifies.

The two notions are, of course, separable. Only by glossing their distinctive subject matters can one arrive at a past at once assertable (as the presupposed is not) and inaccessible (as the historical is not). From this point, the step is small to a past *simpliciter*, replete with all that ever happened, but forever untouchable. The past, however, is nothing to have ontological status independently of event assertions themselves. There are no assertions *about* the past simpliciter unless they are statements about the so-called a priori past, the conceptual framework within which past event statements are made. There are statements about past events, but only after such events have been asserted to have occurred.

The debate, I suggest, is over, for it never reached a genuine point of contention. The thing-in-itself past which Collingwood and Oakeshott denied and the a priori past which they affirmed appear to oppose the Beard-Danto notion of a "past as actuality" which is inaccessible, yet presupposed by calling something evidence or using past-referring terms. The idealists' claim that history is a present world of ideas grew out of the rejection of the thing-in-itself past and perhaps by haste or passion failed to distinguish between what historians do (evaluate present materials *as* evidence) and what they assert (the occurrence of past events). Danto's difficulty, contained in the confusion of a presupposed past and an historical past (rather than a presupposed past and a thing-in-itself past), stems from too uncritical an acceptance of Beard's distinction between "past as actuality" and "past as record." [44] For "all that happened" is what the historian says within the limits of his subject matter and purpose, within the framework of the questions he seeks to answer and the methods by which he answers them. Beard's third category, "history as idea," is, as Danto has correctly pointed out, history as written within a conceptual scheme.[45] That scheme, however, is not a limited theory of linear, cyclical, or chaotic history, which Beard suggested as the only alternatives. Rather, the scheme is the very language in which one makes past event assertions.

The arguments herein, which seek to lift the onus of ontology from event and past event concepts, may leave one feeling empty. Is not history, then, just what we make it—arbitrary, whimsical, insidious? No, not unless one can do away with not only what we consider historians to have correctly said, but as well with the means by which those sayings were made. In treating history as a matter of assent, the positivists made this very error of neglecting the necessity of transforming methodology as well as product, a task monumentally beyond the scope of philosophy.[46] Even George Orwell could not accomplish it. He could keep an ignorant people uneducated by denying them access to any training in even the most rudimentary means of gathering and interpreting evidence. The means by which they are suppressed—mental and physical destruction of those possessing them (e.g., Winston Smith)—leaves open the possibility of their redevelopment.

Or perhaps one has the nagging feeling that there really is a past, a past in which so much happened and about which we know so little. As such, the feeling articulates truly—and is an historical statement. History and the past are not separate rooms, one of which supplies a door to the other: that is only to fall via metaphor into the object language trap again. "Unknown" and "known" are not for history or for any other enterprise wherein event concepts are relevantly used alternatives or complementaries. They are relative termini on multiple judgmental scales which include "plausible" to "implausible," "well-known" to "unknown," "certain" to "uncertain." "There is a past waiting to be discovered. Something must have been going on. It is unreasonable to think otherwise." These are all perfectly good, though vague, historical statements. The best evidence—that it is unreasonable to think otherwise—gives them credence.

But such statements do more than make factual assertions. They express hope, curiosity, an intellectual vacuum wanting to be filled. In this role, such general assertions lead us into the more difficultly mastered techniques of evidential interpretation. They keep historians hard at work when all their pet theories have failed them—as if they ever were dependent upon theory.

Notes

1. The expressions "object language," "event language," and variants upon them are not intended as formal theoretical terms. Rather, their job is to delimit two broad (and perhaps overlapping) classes of categories which we use in speaking of objects and events and in speaking about object and event words. The examples, comments, and especially the argument of section 4 should make the uses of these expressions clear.

2. Michael Oakeshott, *Experience and Its Modes* (Cambridge: Cambridge University Press, 1933), pp. 106–108.

3. Ibid., p. 109.

4. R. G. Collingwood, "The Limits of Historical Knowledge," *Essays in the Philosophy of History*, ed. William Debbins (New York: McGraw-Hill, 1966), pp. 99–101; "The Philosophy of History" in the same collection, pp. 136–138; Collingwood, *The Idea of History* (New York: Oxford University Press, 1956), pp. 251–252.

5. Collingwood, "The Limits of Historical Knowledge," p. 99.

6. Ibid., p. 101. The idealists are not alone in their denial of the past. Attempts have been made to reject idealism's account for just what it got right. For example, in a positivistic piece which the author might not now affirm, Waters agreed with the idealists that, "of course, the correspondence theory of truth is useless in history," but inveighed against idealism's face saving disintegration of objects in favor of thought as the vehicle for history. It would be better to "surrender history, not history as a form of

belief, but the philosopher's ideal of history as confirmable or demonstrable knowledge. Ultimately, we can neither deny nor affirm the reality of the past on any sound logical ground." The possibility of fictionizing history suggests that "in history we can never get beyond assent." For the empiricists, who cannot supply history—as did the realists—with a solid hook into a continuing reality, history becomes a matter of faith. It is, however, in no wise clear precisely to what extent this faith will apply: to facts and names, to evidential objects and documents, to methods of inference and interpretation. There are differences between history and historical fiction which merit separate labels and supply ground for cataloging examples of the latter indifferently with other genres of literature. Forrest may well be the prototype for Sartoris, but the reverse cannot be the case merely by overthrowing present accounts. One must also dispatch all the means by which one makes assertions of and about Forrest and his activities, and that would preclude the prototype relation, let alone its reversal. The same point arises near the end of this study in another context. See Bruce Waters, "The Past and the Historical Past," *Journal of Philosophy* 52 (May 12, 1955): 253–269, especially sections IV and V, but compare his "Historical Narrative," *Southern Journal of Philosophy* 5 (Fall 1967): 206–217.

7. C. A. Beard, "Written History as an Act of Faith," *The Philosophy of History in Our Time*, ed. Hans Meyerhoff (New York: Doubleday, 1959), p. 140.

8. Ibid., pp. 140–141.

9. Ibid., p. 141.

10. Arthur Danto, *Analytical Philosophy of History* (Cambridge: Cambridge University Press, 1965), p. 88.

11. Ibid., pp. 89–91.

12. Ibid., pp. 77–78.

13. Ibid., p. 91.

14. Ibid., p. 115.

15. Ibid., p. 111.

16. Collingwood, "The Philosophy of History," pp. 137–138.

17. Danto, *Analytical Philosophy of History*, p. 226, and Collingwood, *The Idea of History*, pp. 240, 242, and see the entire section, pp. 240–245.

18. Danto, *Analytical Philosophy of History*, p. 91; Collingwood, *The Idea of History*, p. 248.

19. Danto's practice is mostly implicit, as if nothing were wrong with the practice, but see his treatment of narrative sentences in which he uses the expression, "a given event E" (Ibid., p. 146), which is ambiguous. His later treatment of trying to "locate E" via temporal structures (p. 167) and of historical explanations (Chapter 10ff.) more clearly show the opting for E as some event in general.

20. Paul Weiss, *Modes of Being* (Carbondale: Southern Illinois University Press, 1958), pp. 251–367 (propositions 3.67–3.74).

21. The example is stolen from Danto, *Analytical Philosophy of History*, pp. 156–57.

22. Ibid., p. 218.

23. The cop's question, "What happened?" is not equivalent to "What event occurred?" or "With what may I replace E?" His question might be

many things: a *pro forma* order for witnesses to start talking, a request for specific information, a demand for a narrative account of how things got into their present shape, etc. "What happened?" is rarely, if ever, a request for a description *in vacuuo;* rather, its use is occasioned by a change, a surprise, or something out of the ordinary. The expected rarely occasions the question, although a failure to understand how things got to be a certain way may prompt it. However, such a quandary is relieved by showing that things are normal as well as by showing how they came to be.

24. See, e.g., Nagel vs. Rickert in Ernest Nagel, "Some Issues in the Logic of Historical Analysis," *Theories of History*, ed. Patrick Gardiner (New York: The Free Press, 1959), pp. 375–376.

25. In "Colligation and the Writing of History," *Monist* 53 (January 1969): 40–57.

26. See, e.g, Peter Achinstein, *Concepts of Science* (Baltimore: Johns Hopkins University Press, 1968), especially chapter 1; although his rigorous formulations of criterial conditions seem otiose in view of the fact that their contents preclude formalization.

27. This is traditionally said to break down when one reaches the level of group or social concepts.

28. Nagel, "Some Issues in the Logic of Historical Analysis," pp. 375–376.

29. W. H. Dray, " 'Explaining What' in History," *Theories of History*, pp. 403–408.

30. A. J. P. Taylor, *The Origins of the Second World War*, 2nd ed. (New York: Fawcett, 1961), pp. 281ff.

31. The notion of a "basic narrative" seems to have arisen from an empiricist's urge to analyze events, actions, plans, movements all as an empirically verifiable substrata laid over by impure historians with a veneer of values, goals, and other such unverifiable and nonliteral trimmings. History may be a combination of ingredients, but certainly not combined by that simplistic formula.

32. This point helps account for the difficulty philosophers encounter when trying to say what the difference is between past and present and how to tell when one ends and the other begins. Cf. Russell's five minute world and Danto's reply, *Analytical Philosophy of History*, pp. 78–86.

33. The subject of historical evidence, however, has considerable importance on its own ground.

34. Danto, *Analytical Philosophy of History*, pp. 76–78.

35. See Michael Scriven, "Truisms as the Grounds for Historical Explanations," *Theories of History*, especially pp. 463ff.

36. One might even argue that the expression "a wound must have caused the scar" is analytically true, even down to the expression "cause" as here used. The only "causal" question would be what sort of wound (and when, perhaps) made the present particular scar. "Wounds cause scars," when one has the scar and seeks the wound, is not a causal law.

37. In brief, the categories of experience language, i.e., firsthand reporting and personal observation comprise part of the journalistic tool kit, and thus help differentiate that activity from others which cannot employ them.

38. Collingwood, *The Idea of History*, p. 240.

39. Ibid., p. 241, and Danto, *Analytical Philosophy of History*, pp. 122, 125–129.

40. Collingwood, *The Idea of History*, pp. 242, 247.

41. Oakeshott, *Experience and its Modes*, p. 143.

42. Such philosophers as Bergson have favored a bifurcated real vs. known world where continuous reality means uncategorized. However, "continuous" is itself a category.

43. Italics mine.

44. See, for example, Danto's remarks, *Analytical Philosophy of History*, pp. 88–89.

45. Ibid., pp. 99ff., especially pp. 110–111.

46. See above, n. 6.

RESPONSE

John Beversluis

I agree substantially with a great deal of what Professor Cebik says in his paper. He seems to me to be correct in holding that the debate between those who affirm and those who deny that there is an existent past (i.e., between those who affirm and those who deny that there is such a thing as "history as actuality" *in addition to*, and possibly even *presupposed by*, "history as record") is a *philosophical*, rather than an *empirical* one. Furthermore, he seems correct both in his general contention that traditional and contemporary discussions of this problem have been insufficiently attentive to the logic of event concepts, and in his specific thesis that assertions about the occurrence of events require a fundamentally different kind of analysis than do assertions about objects. It is certainly true, as he observes, that if one is to ask intelligibly if there is or can be an existent past, one must understand what it is to say that an event occurred. Although I was persuaded by his arguments to the effect that events are not objects or object-like entities, and that in several important senses statements about an "existent past" are otiose, some sections of his argument remain unclear while others (as developed in his paper) seem inadequate. I will mention those which seem to me most crucial.

The first concerns the expression "the fulfillment of criteria" in his claim that "the use of event concepts is warranted by the fulfillment of criteria." He holds that reference and description apply to events *only after* some assertion of a particular event's occurrence has been made. *Prior* to this the common request to *describe* what happened constitutes merely, i.e., is tantamount to, a request to tell or to say what happened, i.e., a request for the assertion of an event. One result of this, Cebik claims, is that *to assert the occurrence of an event and to use warrantably an event concept* must be taken to be the same thing. The justification of the assertion and the justification of the use are *identical*. In both cases certain criteria have been fulfilled.

This might be a promising suggestion provided that we were clear on the precise relation between our being able to recognize something as an event on the one hand and our being in possession of criteria for the term "event" on the other. According to Cebik, with regard to event concepts there is nothing of concern except the criteria to be fulfilled in order for there to be a warranted assertion of an event. That is to say, the use of the event concepts depends in no way upon a "preassertorial reference." But it seems to me that, if we are not in possession of criteria which warrant our calling something an "event," how will we recognize one? On the other hand, do we not need to know the various sorts of things that count as events *prior* to our having criteria for events in order, for example, to be able to assert, as Cebik does, that it is not possible to produce a *general* definition of events or that events do not share common essential characteristics? In short, though it might be plausible to argue that the use of event concepts does not presuppose a preassertorial reference to some object-like entity, it does *not* follow that *merely to assert* the occurrence of an event and to use *warrantably* an event concept are the same thing unless one adds to assert *truly*[1] the occurrence of an event. What, therefore, in Cebik's analysis, distinguishes true from false assertions, i.e., what distinguishes the warranted from the unwarranted use of event concepts?

If Cebik is correct in his contention that there need be no fundamental level of events to serve as the ultimate referent of the event concepts, what is there in his analysis to place a limitation upon the number of ways in which one could describe an event? Even if events are not complexes, and furthermore, even if not everything in a complex is involved in, or relevant to, the assertion of the occurrence of any event, why could not what "happened" be described or accounted for, or asserted to have taken place, in a wide variety of ways? One can, I think, go further. Given Cebik's rejection of the distinction between a description of E and E, in conjunction with this contention that there is no referent whatsoever which provides a univocal meaning for "same" in the expression "the same event," why could not one argue that to hold out for a wide variety of ways of asserting what happened is quite compatible with his view?

Finally, if, as Cebik concludes, there is no such thing as an event-in-itself, but only a conceptual framework within which past statements are made, what meaning *are* we to assign to the term "event" in the question: "Do events occur?" a question Cebik answers affirmatively? Having deprived events of "ontological status," Cebik denies that history is thereby rendered arbitrary, whimsical, and insidious. This claim might be defensible. That is, it may *not* require an ontological analysis in order to retain content for terms such as "history," "the past," or "events." But has Cebik's analysis provided us with an adequate alternative? I do not think so. Thus, the chief merit of his paper, viz., to have pointed out some important disanalogies between event language and object language, may well be the source of one of its most significant obscurities. Given such a state of affairs, we ought to thank him for the former and ask for more light about the latter.

Note

1. In making this point I am not, of course, requesting that Professor Cebik provide us with a full-blown "theory of truth." I am merely arguing that the *mere* assertion of an event is not the same thing as a *warranted use* of an event concept. A *warranted use* is a *true* assertion. A false assertion, then, would presumably be an *unwarranted* use of the concept of an event.

INDEX OF NAMES

2230 1